Critical Race Theory and *Bamboozled*

FILM THEORY IN PRACTICE

Critical Race Theory and *Bamboozled*

ALESSANDRA RAENGO

Bloomsbury Academic
An imprint of Bloomsbury Publishing Plc

B L O O M S B U R Y
NEW YORK • LONDON • OXFORD • NEW DELHI • SYDNEY

Bloomsbury Academic
An imprint of Bloomsbury Publishing Plc

1385 Broadway
New York
NY 10018
USA

50 Bedford Square
London
WC1B 3DP
UK

www.bloomsbury.com

BLOOMSBURY and the Diana logo are trademarks of Bloomsbury Publishing Plc

First published 2016

Library of Congress Cataloging-in-Publication Data
Names: Raengo, Alessandra, author.
Title: Critical race theory and *Bamboozled* / Alessandra Raengo.
Description: New York : Bloomsbury Academic, 2016. |
Series: Film theory in practice |
Includes bibliographical references and index.
Identifiers: LCCN 2016009703 (print) | LCCN 2016010323 (ebook) |
ISBN 9781501305801 (hardback) | ISBN 9781501305818 (ePDF) |
ISBN 9781501305832 (ePub)
Subjects: LCSH: Bamboozled (Motion picture) | African Americans in motion
pictures. | Race in motion pictures. | Racism in motion pictures. | Race. |
BISAC: PERFORMING ARTS / Film & Video / History & Criticism. |
SOCIAL SCIENCE / Ethnic Studies / General.
Classification: LCC PN1997.B2435 R33 2016 (print) | LCC PN1997.B2435 (ebook) |
DDC 791.43/72–dc23 LC record available at http://lccn.loc.gov/2016009703

ISBN: HB: 978-1-5013-0580-1
       PB: 978-1-5013-0579-5
       ePUB: 978-1-5013-0583-2
       ePDF: 978-1-5013-0581-8

Series: Film Theory in Practice

Cover design: Alice Marwick
Cover image © Stills from 'Bamboozled' (2000) © 40 ACRES & A MULE / NEW LINE /
THE KOBAL COLLECTION / LEE, DAVID

Typeset by Newgen Knowledge Works (P) Ltd., Chennai, India

To Margot,
for her unique graces

CONTENTS

ACKNOWLEDGMENTS

I am very grateful to Todd McGowan for asking me to write this book, to Adam Cottrel for suggesting my name to Todd, and to Hugh Manon and Paul Einstein for green-lighting my proposal. Todd has been phenomenally supportive and kind throughout the process. I particularly appreciate his openness toward the more experimental traits of my writing.

My intellectual life has benefited from a good number of companions and interlocutors: Brian Price and Meghan Sutherland, Angelo Restivo, Jennifer Barker, Louis Ruprecht, Eddie Chambers, Marina Peterson, Kris Cannon, Drew Ayers, and Jay Derby, as well as from many conversations with Lauren Cramer, Kristin Juarez, Cameron Kunzleman, and Chris Hunt in the context of our common work for the *liquid blackness* research group.

I owe a theoretical debt to a number of scholars cited in this book, including some I have known for a long time or I have only recently had the fortune to meet, including Anne Cheng, Kara Keeling, Derek Conrad Murray, Robert Stam, Ed Guerrero, Manthia Diawara, Paula Massood, Keith Harris, Michael Gillepsie, and Agustin Zarzosa.

Charles "Chip" Linscott and Michele Prettyman Beverly have been absolutely vital to the completion of this book. I met Chip and Michele at the very beginning of my academic life as an assistant professor and I know I have learned from them just as much as they have learned from me. This book owes a lot to their attentive, patient, and acute input. They worked closely with me to fine-tune my pedagogical choices (Michele) and make my prose much more effective (Chip). I appreciate their (and their families') generosity in keeping up with the furious pace of my writing. This book would simply not have happened without their committed, gracious, and brilliant contribution.

I am gifted with a great group of nonacademic friends who routinely put up with me and my, at times, insane schedule: Juliet, Marshall, and Terry; Mike and Melissa; Danielle and Jason; Greg; and many others. There is a chance they don't really know how grounding and rewarding their friendship has been for me. And so has been the support of my siblings back in Italy and particularly my sister Laura.

A number of sections of this book have been written in bars. That particular ambient noise inspires me. I am grateful to many bartenders who have put up with my conspicuous laptop or my annoying stacks of papers, but I want to single out Joshua Collins, from the Trackside Bar, in Decatur, Georgia, who always, always made me feel absolutely welcome.

My daughter Margot truly rocks. She is only twelve, but her daily life has been unavoidably affected by my writing projects ever since she was a baby. She witnesses my struggles, endures my constant working, and listens to some of my conceptual dilemmas. She knows the sacrifices of academic life but respects my choices. I am forever grateful for her grace.

Finally, too many black lives unnecessarily lost have been haunting this writing. This book is inspired by the need and desire to make this carnage cease once and for all.

I have worked through some conceptual sections of this book in previous writing, most prominently "Optic Black: Blackness as Phantasmagoria," in *Beyond Blackface: Africana Images in the US Media*, ed. Akil Houston (Dubuque: Kendall Hunt Publishing, 2010, 2nd edition); "Reification, Reanimation, and the Money of the Real," *World Picture* no. 7 (2012); and *On the Sleeve of the Visual: Race as Face Value* (Hanover, NH: Dartmouth College Press, 2013). I thank Christopher Minz for his assistance with research for the book.

Introduction

The term "Critical Race Theory" emerged in the context of legal studies in the 1980s but has since come to indicate, more broadly, scholarship from several disciplines in the humanities that focuses on issues of race. When scholars in African American studies, philosophy, literary studies, performance studies, cultural studies, women's studies, queer studies, art history, and social and political theory put race at the center of their inquiry, they are doing Critical Race Theory. In this sense, Critical Race Theory can be understood as "critical theory" *about* race, but with some qualifications: while drawing on many canonical formations in critical theory proper—such as psychoanalysis, semiotics, Marxist theory, and phenomenology, among others—Critical Race Theory also challenges these same formations to reconfigure some of their assumptions and methods so that they can fully account for race. Finally, in yet another sense, Critical Race Theory refers to the way African American and black diasporic thought has dialogued with, as well as distanced itself from, critical theory and Western philosophy in order to articulate a specific black philosophical stance.

In film, media, and visual culture studies, "Critical Race Theory" does not have an established canonical presence and therefore the term is still cautiously adopted.[1] Scholarship that focuses on race and blackness in the cinema is increasingly described as "black film studies," a label that, in turn, maintains a tension between scholarship *about* "black film" and *black* scholarship about the cinema. When this scholarship taps into the larger body of work just described, and especially when it addresses the intersection between race and the cinema, it too is performing Critical Race Theory.

One common trait of all these strands of Critical Race Theory is the commitment to *start from*, rather than *arrive at*, issues of race. This means that they demand a redefinition of the very terms within which race is normally discussed and do not tolerate theoretical or practical segregation, whereby race is a legitimate topic of scholarship only in dedicated environments, or as a special case, or in a liberal spirit of inclusivity, or very uncomfortably and, as recently argued in a dedicated section of *Cinema Journal*, only on the last page of the syllabus.

There is no question in my mind that the film that performs the theoretical work of putting Critical Race Theory *into practice* is Spike Lee's *Bamboozled* (2000), as the interdisciplinary breadth of its critical reception makes clear. The film, in fact, has been read in a large variety of disciplinary contexts and, in some cases, it has offered a provocative contribution to some of the questions posed in those fields. *Bamboozled* is central to visual culture studies, for instance, for the way it stages the meeting point between visual and material culture; it is exemplary of "thing theory" for its commitment to the material culture of race; it contributes to the reflection on the digital turn because of the experimental use of consumer grade digital video cameras alongside Super 16 mm footage for the sequences dedicated to the minstrel show; and it has been regarded as foreseeing the rise of reality television because of the way it theorizes the relationship between media audiences and blackness. Furthermore, *Bamboozled*'s reflection on the relationship between blackness and the commodity form and its circular and recursive temporality contributes to theories of capital; finally, its challenge to the distinction between subject and object, human and nonhuman, and the strategic way in which the film employs object movement can be seen to offer a critique of some recent trends in contemporary philosophy that advance a non-anthropocentric stance, such as object oriented ontology and speculative realism.

In other words, *Bamboozled* is not simply a good case study but a text that stages a series of theoretical interventions in various strands of Critical Race Theory, ultimately taking a position in the most radical argument to emerge from this field, that is, that the question of blackness is an ontological question. In Western philosophy "ontology" describes what pertains to the nature of Being. Yet there are objects that can come into being at a specific historical moment. Blackness is one of them. Because New World slavery produced an entity that was not part of the human fold—the slave as a "subperson" living in a condition of "social death"—it also created blackness as a problem of Being.[2] Captives entered the slave ship as Africans and exited as blacks, and the blackness produced by this transition as the mark of their captivity unavoidably puts the very concept and boundaries of the human in crisis, as well as troubling the community of humans—the *world*—we live in. When, under the pretext of blackness, a human being is framed as something entirely different, this means that blackness produces a position that is outside the purview of humanity and yet still central to its definition. Thus any scholarly field that addresses issues of race and blackness has to, sooner or later, confront the question of *political ontology* posed by its very object. It has to reflect on what it takes for the Black to be acknowledged *as* a subject who is fully part of the human community.

Consistent with that, this book too has to begin with the gesture that gives rise to the "critical moment" about race in legal studies: the critique of color blindness, which, in disciplinary terms, means the critique of the very exclusion of race from the scholarly conversation. This very exclusionary act ("for whites only . . .") creates the question of the political ontology of black existence, the partition whereby black lives do not count as other lives. In other words, how does one talk about black people if blackness emerged in antithesis to the idea of the "person"? How does one talk about black lives if what is black about them is precisely what is not protected within the very notion of human life?

These questions take us, at least apparently, quite far from the cinema but not far at all from the purpose of this book, which is informed by these profound questions, even when they are not addressed directly. It does so precisely because *Bamboozled* itself continues to keep these issues in focus by putting pressure on a number of ontological distinctions in Western thought: the distinctions between subject and object, person and thing, human and nonhuman, and animate and inanimate, among others. Indeed, *Bamboozled* is so forward-looking and theoretically rich that I have decided to let it guide most of the structural choices of the book, including the choice to focus squarely on blackness (as opposed to other forms of racial otherness) as the fundamental racial paradigm in US society and culture.

Critical Race Theory in legal studies

Within the field of legal studies where it first originates, "Critical Race Theory" (which henceforth I will refer to as CRT to distinguish it from the larger understanding of Critical Race Theory as encompassing insights from all three strands) designates the scholarship and activism produced primarily as a critique of the color-blind legislation that emerged from the Civil Rights era. The story of how a group of scholars and graduate students identified their work and commitment under the label "Critical Race Theory" is well documented. In 1980, Derrick Bell, author of *Race, Racism, and American Law*, left Harvard University to head the University of Oregon School of Law. At Harvard, Bell had been teaching race-conscious law classes, so students of color requested a minority hire as Bell's replacement. The Harvard administration resisted, on the grounds that there was no minority scholar qualified for the position. In protest, the law students organized an alternative course on race and the law, which drew the support of several sympathetic Harvard faculty. This class was the first institutional manifestation of the Critical Race Theory movement.

On the left of the legal field, Critical Race Theory emerges in conversation with Critical Legal Studies (CLS), sharing with it a critique of the way in which the law constructs and preserves power relations, perpetuates ideology, and maintains hegemony. Yet, CLS's lack of focus on racial power sharpens CRT's reaction to the idea of the law as an "apolitical mediator of racial conflict" and its critique of the idea of formal equality and color blindness governing civil rights discourse.[3] Dissatisfied with a framework that does not allow for the fact of structural inequalities, CRT investigates how the law has historically participated in the construction of race and in the maintenance of a system of white supremacy.

Thus, CRT has a defined birthplace and institutional context—Harvard University in the early 1980s—an established roster of scholars (Derrick Bell, Richard Delgado, Neil Gotanda, Kimberlé Williams Crenshaw, Thomas Kendall, and Jean Stefancic among the most known), a consolidated narrative of development, and a series of tenets. This body of work has addressed cultural issues, and, occasionally and tangentially, questions of aesthetics, but it has had a very limited engagement with film.

Overall, CRT espouses the following theses. Racism is ordinary; it is not made of extraordinarily vicious acts, but rather of assumptions that underlie quotidian practices and interactions. No racial progress occurs unless there is convergence of material interests ("interest convergence" thesis), which was the motor behind civil rights legislation in the 1950s and 1960s. Indeed, very little imagination of social change was necessary at the time to set the civil rights legislation in motion, and there is still a remarkable continuity between the segregationist and civil rights regimes.

Even though there is an expectation that racial categories are unchangeable, the legal construction of race has historically been very flexible, and groups have been racialized differently at different times ("differential racialization" thesis). In turn, racialization is a process constantly repeated in order to be secured. CRT is deliberately antiessentialist in the sense of recognizing that no person has one stable and single identity, and it has introduced the idea of intersectionality in order to address multiple axes of oppression along race, class, gender, and sexuality, for example, and the specific ways they combine in given circumstances.[4] CRT is also deliberately partial to the minority position, which it considers the most competent to speak about oppression, particularly because redress of historical and structural inequalities can only be achieved if racial injury is allowed to become an object of grievance ("voice-of-color" thesis).

CRT's main critique, however, is directed at color blindness because it promotes a merely formal equality, which alone cannot address structural racism, but instead attends to only the most blatant forms of discrimination. CRT critiques civil rights discourse for having adopted a formal understanding of race wherein black and white are handled as two symmetrical categories rather than socioculturally or historically shaped identities.

Critical Race Theory as critical theory *about* race

In a broader sense, though, Critical Race Theory presses canonical approaches in critical theory to address the question of race as fundamental to their concerns. It can be described as the theoretical engagement with the centrality of race to humanistic inquiry. Put more strongly, it investigates a central antagonism between race and the humanities to the extent that, as an ontological position, the Black is not only excluded from the sphere of the human, but also its opposite.

Scholarship that most radically expresses this position moves from the view that slavery produced an ontological violence that still affects black existence. This is because the defining condition of the slave is not captivity or coerced labor, but rather, as Orlando Patterson argued, "social death": first, the slave has no recognized existence outside of the master and is therefore a "social nonperson"; and second, she is alienated, at birth, from any and all rights. The slave is perpetually susceptible to violence, and has neither kinship structure nor any relationships that must be recognized. She exists outside of (human) relations.

One consequence of this condition is the paradoxical situation whereby black life is lived in conditions of *social* or *political* "death." Another is that there is no relationship available with blackness that does not occur within the terms of its use. The master has ownership over everything the slave does, including his/her enjoyment. Another consequence is black *fungibility*, not only because the slave shares the status of the commodity, which is by nature replaceable and disposable, but also because blackness has tremendous metaphorical properties: it becomes a foil for the master and the nation to understand themselves.[5]

This condition whereby the slave's ontological status continues to secure his/her erasure is explained by Frantz Fanon's description of the lack of ontological ground for the native in the colonial situation. "Ontology," he writes, "does not permit us to understand the being of the Black. For not only must the black man be black; but he must be black in relation to the white man."[6] On one hand, the Manichean colonial regime demands nothing less than "absolute substitution" in order for the native to enter the fold of the human: the native, he explains, does not want to, nor can he, "become" the settler, but rather must replace him entirely. On the other hand, the native exists only in terms of comparison to the white settler, and never in his own terms. He is always outside, below, or underneath the human community. How is it possible, from this perspective, to discuss black life, or advocate for black lives as lives worth loving and protecting?

Moving from this impulse to address the constant disqualification of black life and the lack of positive ontology for blackness, Critical Race Theory, in this larger interdisciplinary sense, is programmatically committed to redress the relegation of race studies to dedicated departments or particular institutional formations and to be partial to race instead, while claiming its centrality in a number of academic fields. It therefore seeks to begin its reflection from the standpoint of race by leveraging the epistemic advantage of the disenfranchised.

Critical Race Theory and film studies

Given the radical questions posed by the first two strands of Critical Race Theory, what does it mean to think about Critical Race Theory in relation to film studies or *as* film studies? The almost simultaneous publication of a special issue of *Black Scholar* devoted to the question of black lives (and the way in which black studies can properly address their continued fragility) and an "In-focus" section of *Cinema Journal* on the status of "black film theory" can help answer this question.[7] Read alongside one another they effectively indicate how the continued marginalization of black film theory and black studies parallels the ongoing dismissal of blackness as an ontological problem for Western thought. Thus, Critical Race Theory enters film studies when the latter embraces blackness in all its theoretical potential, including the possibility to legitimately pose an ontological question about both the image and the human.

When Fanon talks about the failure of "ontology" to account for the Black, he also wants to criticize the inadequacy of existing philosophical frameworks to really understand the existence of the Black. Phenomenology does not fully explain the experience of a body marked by race, he argues; Marxism does not understand that in the colonial setting the base is the superstructure and it combines with race in specific ways: you are rich because you are white and white because you are rich; psychoanalysis, which he practiced when working in a mental hospital in Algiers, has not yet figured out how to understand that the colonial relation is a form of colonization of the psyche; and so on. Film studies has to be similarly brought to the task. Like most critical theory, it is "white" by default and illusorily self-contained. The implied subject of the cinema is still racially unmarked, "black film" is still handled as a genre apart, and when one does Critical Race Theory through film one still has to describe it as *black* film studies.

The default tendency in film studies is to approach issues of race as a question of representation, that is, with a focus on race as *content*. Yet, the provocation that Critical Race Theory brings to film studies is to conceptualize race in the cinema in terms of *form*; in other words, to think of blackness both as a challenge for film form and as a reservoir of surplus expressivity, mobility, affect, and pathos that has benefited film aesthetics since the cinema's inception. Finally, blackness presents a challenge to our understanding of the ontology of the photographic image given that historically photography has built its truth-value and effect of transparency on the display of the black body. Blackness, therefore, concerns film studies at a fundamental level because, in some way, the Black is always already an image.

For this reason the trajectory outlined by the very appearance and use of the term "Critical Race Theory," from its origin in legal studies to its deployment in a wider interdisciplinary context, passes through another disciplinary formation before reaching the cinema: visual culture studies. A reason for this is the attachment of US law to the understanding of race in visual terms. From the sanctioning of skin color as the natural signifier of racial difference in *Plessy v. Ferguson*, which established Jim Crow as a visual regime of segregation, to the doctrine of color blindness and the concept of the color line, race in US law appears as an unavoidably visual formation. In fact, as I will discuss later, both the question of the color line and its imagined overcoming—the idea of color blindness— entail two complicated visual culture projects that have to be addressed as such. They are examples of what visual culture studies takes as one of its objects of focus, that is, the visual construction of the social sphere.[8]

It is from within the disciplinary formation of visual culture studies that W. J. T. Mitchell has argued for another way to perform Critical Race Theory, that is, the need to think of *race as a medium*, something we see through, like a frame, window, screen, or lens; a series of "cognitive and conceptual filters" to manage and organize human differences; a costume, a mask, or performance; and a way to *mediate* between a variety of concepts such as nature and culture, fantasy and reality, and concepts of space and time. "Race" in this sense is so expansive and so resilient that "there is nothing else in the world, or in language, that can do all that we ask race to do for us."[9]

Plan of the book

In addressing these issues, I follow three leads. The first is legal studies. I begin by introducing and then building upon three of the tenets espoused by CRT, that is, the critique of the ideology of color blindness attending to civil rights legislation, the claim that formal equality does not translate into social equality, and the claim that racism is ordinary and structural. I initially focus most on the idea of *form* because that is the vehicle through which blackness first enters US law in the context of the ontological scandal of slavery—that is, the collapsed distinction between subject and object, human and commodity—and because of the way race enters the cinema as a problem for and of form. I then address color blindness as an impossible visual culture project, and the ordinariness of racism through scholarship that deals with racial intimacy and the "erotic" life of racism. I focus on the sensorial construction of race, that is, how race is *made* and how it is made to *make sense*, to show how, through this individual and collective construction, blackness becomes something very similar to a *thing*.

My second lead comes from visual culture studies. I show how the idea of formal equality depends on an optical model of race, whereby blackness is primarily a visual problem that can be resolved through visual means. To complicate that, I introduce other ways to think about the cooperation of all the senses in the construction of race and how this fact acknowledges more intimacy, contact, and, ultimately, melancholia in the relation with the other.

Moving then into more disciplinary-specific questions about "representations of race"—which assumes that truthful, correct, and authentic representations can positively impact the lives of black subjects—I offer an overview of various ways of understanding stereotypes in order to pay attention to their complexity as *scenes* of subject formation, desire, and incorporation, as well as how they stage a meeting point between visual and material culture. In other words, prompted by *Bamboozled* itself, I show how stereotypes can be seen as both pictures and things.

My third lead comes from the ontological question posed within black studies and shows how blackness puts under duress notions of time, history, subjecthood, and objecthood. The very object of race or "black" film studies is at stake here, a problem that "white" film theory does not have, in the sense that it does not have to justify its purview. Twenty years ago, Stuart Hall asked, "What is this 'black' in black popular culture?" We are still nowhere close to an answer.[10]

Overall, the purpose of this book is not to review the history of "black film studies," but to harness helpful and lasting analytical tools that are reflected in, inspired by, and comprised under the label "Critical Race Theory" in its broadest sense. Thus, it becomes an opportunity not only to think about how one might perform what in the conclusion I describe as "critical race analysis," but also, even more profoundly, to think about what might be some of the moves that are necessary for race to be fully part of the conversation in film studies.

I have framed this discussion of the relationship between Critical Race Theory and film studies mostly from the point of view of contemporary theory. This is partly in response to the way *Bamboozled* challenges many disciplinary formations to think ahead and beyond more traditional scholarship. Since the interdisciplinary breath of Critical Race Theory does not afford the opportunity to provide a linear historical narrative I have organized the book around "primal scenes," that is, "classical" passages or texts, and case studies where a variety of approaches come together around similar questions. These are the points of contact between legal discourse, critical theory *about* race, and scholarship developed within black studies. Their exemplary nature makes them pedagogically effective. Overall, I have adopted an "object-oriented" pedagogy that, when possible, uses media objects (for instance, skits from the *Chappelle's Show* or specific film sequences) to explain theory in a way that can be adapted to the reading of other objects, as I exemplify in the conclusion. Finally, I have incorporated some pedagogical exercises to show how a critical race analysis may be practically performed in a classroom setting.

Notes

1   An attempt at integrating Critical Race Theory and film studies is offered by Gerald Sim who, in *The Subject of Film and Race: Retheorizing Politics, Ideology, and Cinema* (New York: Bloomsbury Publishing, 2014), describes his approach as "critical race film studies."

2   "Subperson" is the concept advanced by Charles Mills in *The Racial Contract* (Ithaca: Cornell University Press, 1997), while the definition of slavery as "social death" was formulated by Orlando Patterson, in *Slavery and Social Death: A Comparative Study* (Cambridge, MA: Harvard University Press, 1982).

3   Kimberlé Crenshaw, Neil Gotanda, Peller Gary, and Thomas Kendall, eds, *Critical Race Theory: The Key Writings That Formed the Movement* (New York: New Press, 1995), xxv. See also Richard Delgado and Jean Stefancic, eds, *Critical Race Theory: The Cutting Edge* (Philadelphia: Temple University Press, 2000); and Richard Delgado and Jean Stefancic, *Critical Race Theory: An Introduction* (New York: NYU Press, 2012).

4   The term "intersectionality" was coined by Kimberlé Crenshaw in "Demarginalizing the Intersection of Race and Sex: A Black Feminist Critique of Antidiscrimination Doctrine, Feminist Theory and Antiracist Politics," *University of Chicago Legal*

Forum (1989): 139–67, to challenge the fact that the law considers race and gender discrimination separately. In *Black Feminist Thought: Knowledge, Consciousness and the Politics of Empowerment* (Boston: Unwin Hyman, 1990), Patricia Hill Collins introduces the idea of "matrix of domination" to refer to how these intersecting forms of oppression are organized. Even though the term was coined in 1989, several older black feminist texts were central to this line of thinking. Among them are Angela Davis, *Women, Race, and Class* (New York: Vintage, 1983); Barbara Smith, ed., *Home Girls: A Black Feminist Anthology* (New York: Kitchen Table/Women of Color Press, 1983); and bell hooks, *Ain't I a Woman? Black Women and Feminism* (Boston: South End Press, 1981).

5   The following texts are central to this conversation often described under the umbrella of "Afro-Pessimism": Saidiya Hartman, *Scenes of Subjection: Terror, Slavery, and Self-Making in Nineteenth-Century America* (New York: Oxford University Press, 1997); Saidiya Hartman and Frank B. Wilderson, III, "The Position of the Unthought," *Qui Parle* 13, no. 2 (2003): 183–201; Jared Sexton, *Amalgamation Schemes: Antiblackness and the Critique of Multiracialism* (Minneapolis: University of Minnesota Press, 2008); Frank B. Wilderson, III, *Red, White & Black: Cinema and the Structure of Us Antagonisms* (Durham, NC: Duke University Press, 2010); Jared Sexton, "The Social Life of Social Death: On Afro-Pessimism and Black Optimism," *InTensions* 5 (2011): 1–47; and Fred Moten's critical response in "Blackness and Nothingness (Mysticism in the Flesh)," *South Atlantic Quarterly* 112, no. 4 (2013): 737–80.

6   Frantz Fanon, *Black Skins, White Masks*, trans. Richard Philcox (New York: Grove Press, 2008), 90.

7   Alexander Weheliye, ed., Special issue on "Black Studies on Black Life," *The Black Scholar* 44, no. 2 (2014); and Beretta E. Smith-Shomade, Racquel Gates, and Miriam J. Petty, eds, "In-Focus: African American Caucus," *Cinema Journal* 53, no. 4 (2014): 121–63.

8   The field of visual culture studies has taken shape over the past three decades as a shift occurring in a variety of disciplines, such as art history, film and media studies, cultural studies, literary studies, and material culture studies, among others. It is thus

a vast interdisciplinary field concerned with the examination of the image culture we live in, the way in which images offer forms of mediation and function themselves as media, as well as the visual construction of the social sphere. See Nicholas Mirzoeff, *An Introduction to Visual Culture*, 2nd ed. (London and New York: Routledge, 2009); and W. J. T. Mitchell, *What Do Pictures Want? The Lives and Loves of Images* (Chicago and London: University of Chicago Press, 2005).

9 W. J. T. Mitchell, *Seeing through Race* (Cambridge, MA: Harvard University Press, 2012), 14. Mitchell expands a similar statement by philosopher Anthony Appiah in "The Uncompleted Argument: Du Bois and the Illusion of Race," *Critical Inquiry* 12, no. 1 (1985): 21–37.

10 Stuart Hall, "What Is This 'Black' in Black Popular Culture?," in *Black Popular Culture*, ed. Gina Dent (Seattle, WA: Bay Press, 1992), 21–32.

CHAPTER ONE

Critical Race Theory

Formal equality and the problem of the "color-blind"

Any piece of scholarship about race will have to explicitly or implicitly justify its own existence in the larger world. Why talk about race? Why risk being divisive by bringing it up? In many ways, what W. E. B. Du Bois predicted as the main problem of the twentieth century, that is, the problem of the "color line," has now become the problem of the color-*blind*.[1] As much as we can represent race as a purely discursive construct, its grip on real lives has not ceased. As much as we might desire to no longer "see" race, or "see through" it, there is a "thereness" to the racial body and the very idea of racial difference that cannot be dismissed. The reality of racial discrimination and the continued devaluation of black lives still demand accounting.

Neil Gotanda identifies four ways the Supreme Court has addressed race: in terms of status, culturally, historically, and formally. Status-race is the idea of race as an indication of (inferior) social status.[2] Culture-race is a way to describe the cultural specificity of different racial groups, and historical-race focuses on the history of racial oppression. For CRT, formal-race is the most problematic framework because it regards "black" and "white" as symmetrical categories unattached to social categories and, consequently, as intrinsically reversible and therefore equal. Formal-race holds that nothing in the concept of blackness and whiteness suggests dominance or subordination. Equality then becomes a question of symmetry, a symmetry that CRT shows is not actual—cannot be put into action—but rather *counterfactual*, that is, speculative, hypothetical, and tied to the ability to imagine the tables turned.

Formal-race adopts what we might consider a fundamentally structuralist logic that resonates with Ferdinand de Saussure's understanding of language as a system of differences without positive terms, or a system of oppositions that acquire content only by virtue of their relation. Thus, formal equality manages the relationship between categories that are considered fundamentally empty. Yet, this evacuation of social, cultural, and historical content is in itself a product of privilege.

CRT has emphasized how Civil Rights legislation treats racial power as an aberration, rather than a systemic problem, and treats racism as irrational and subjective, rather than structural. This is because formal equality can only prohibit *explicit* racial exclusion. Consequently, only discrete and identifiable acts of prejudice, rather than systemic inequalities, can be counted as acts of racism. Thus, the sphere of the everyday is kept entirely beyond the purview of the law. Against that, Critical Race Theory insists that racism is systemic and an everyday occurrence.

Formal equality is partly fueled by a contractual imagination, the idea that a common agreement makes the subjects equal. Similarly, equality is based on concepts of *likeness*: alike people should be treated alike. Yet, there is a difference between equal treatment and treatment *as equal*, a difference that the idea of formal equality cannot address. As a result, color blindness is often coupled with ideologies of equal opportunity and can be leveraged for both conservative and liberal ends. For both, color blindness is supposed to empty the category of race of any content and thus return whatever injury, grief, or grievance to a symmetrical difference in the social map. In the law, color blindness demands "racial nonrecognition," which means that race is the thing that has to be denied, the structural inequality that has to be evacuated in order for the *form* of an equal exchange to appear. Color blindness delivers this pristine form.

For both conservative and liberal positions, the opposite of color blindness is racism. This means that any time race is given a content (it is attached to a history of oppression, for example) or, at its most extreme, any time race is even *discussed*, this very fact is considered an expression of racism. For visual culture scholar W. J. T. Mitchell, race is the consequence rather than the cause of racism, and if one eliminates race from the conversation, one will be left without a way to discuss racism at all. Thus, even though it is still always evoked as the surest antidote against racial discrimination, color blindness is ultimately another way to express an investment in *formal* equality without a commitment to *social* equality.[3]

Formal equality cannot deliver social equality because it is based on an assumption of symmetry. In turn, the idea of symmetry presupposes the possibility of a real or imagined exchange. Theoretically, the tables could be turned at any moment, and all parties would still be treated equally. Equal things exchange equally. And, if the opposite is true, that is, that things that exchange equally are equal, then color blindness also propels and justifies the conflation between formal equality and *equation*. It is because of its formality that the equality espoused by color-blind ideology becomes equation and thus is implicated in the logic of capitalist exchange. In fact, the type of "form" that is always about exchange is the *commodity form*, which haunts many appearances of blackness in the law.

Legal form and commodity form

This haunting happens in part because of the specific dimensions of racial slavery and in part due to the very characteristics of *form*. The commodity form is central to slave law. The slave is the (unrecognized) human in the "form" of a commodity. Or, as Harriet Beecher Stowe's original subtitle for *Uncle Tom's Cabin* put it—"The Man Who Was a Thing"—the slave is a thing with a biography. Personhood, instead, is defined as the effect of property rights on one's own person; in other words, as having possession of oneself. The entanglement of race and personhood—the racialization of identity, as CRT calls it—pivots around the institution of slavery from the beginning. In the founding era, property is understood not simply as an external relationship to an object one owns but also as that to which one attaches value, or to which one has rights. Human rights (such as freedom, liberty, and immunity), for example, are a type of property. Whiteness is the attribute that guarantees freedom—indeed, the impossibility of being enslaved—and freedom is a form of property. Whiteness, therefore, means having property rights in one's personhood. Freedom is thus a function of having personhood, defined as having possession of oneself. This is why W. E. B. Du Bois described whiteness as a "wage" for the free worker.

Blackness, on the contrary, *presumes* one's status as property. While the Representation Clause in the Constitution defines the slave as three-fifth of a human being, the form of the person slowly begins to appear in slave law, strictly for the purposes of accountability. In the Fugitive Slave Law of 1850, which required the extradition of the fugitive slaves arriving in the north, the slave assumes the form of a person insofar as she owes labor to her master. Only when she escapes does the slave become visible *as* a person. It is the economic exchange, the transaction itself that figures personhood, and, only consequently, the subject involved in the transaction.

It is at the formal level that the person takes shape in the law. Once personhood is defined formally in this way, it can also be extended to entities that are not people; the corporation, for example, becomes legally recognized as an artificial person with a body and will under the Supreme Court decision in *Santa Clara v. Southern Pacific Railroad* (1885), which leveraged the Fourteenth Amendment protecting the rights of recently emancipated slaves. The corporation thus hijacks the legal space created to protect the recognition of the *natural* personhood of the slave in order to create an *artificial* one.[4]

The form of the person is also central to intellectual property law as a way to protect property rights in aspects of the person that were previously considered inalienable. In the context of increasing means of mechanical reproduction (the printing press, photography, the gramophone, and so on), copyright law helped define the right to one's personality by encouraging an even stronger distinction between a personal right and a property right: one is inalienable and the other is exchangeable and subject to the market. These processes of alienation triggered by the formal notion of the person are part of a systemic confusion between person and property; they are the specters of the ontological scandal of slavery surviving in the text of the law.

As these examples indicate, *form* has a generative function in the law. Form is a causal principle because every case has to be judged in analogy with another. Thus, the form similar legal cases have previously assumed regulates how things are seen in the present and how they might be seen in the future. Ultimately, form possesses agency because, in the law, analogy is a form of causality.

Form in the law can also be a principle of inertia, in the sense of hindering, rather than facilitating, change. Thus, the question of form becomes a practical issue when CRT scholars are confronted with the difficulty of changing a system that, by structure, is poorly equipped to redress certain types of wrongs. In fact, once the structure of the law or specific categories within it takes form, it replicates in the legal realm in the manner of DNA in biology. Form can be an agent of proliferation of a continued sameness, and, therefore, it can become a way to maintain the status quo.

Form also has the potential to act as a principle of translation because it can mediate between different things, so long as they can be compared in some fundamental way, or so long as they have something in common that can be exchanged. This is more specifically a characteristic of the commodity form, which is the type of form that is always about exchange.

Consider this: Marx begins *Capital* with a discussion of the commodity to show that the commodity is a microcosm of the entire structure of capital. A commodity is a man-made thing that possesses a use value and an exchange value. The use value is qualitative, while the exchange value is quantitative. When two qualitatively different things exchange in the market, it is because they have something in common, an entity that is the product of abstraction from their individuality and specificity. Marx identifies this commonality as value, that is, abstract human labor. This seeming transformation of a qualitative difference into a quantitative sameness is a change in *form*: an object of utility now appears as an object of exchange. Therefore, the commodity form is a *mode of appearance* of a thing and thus a *principle of visibility*, but it is also a switch point, or a *scene of exchange*, in which a qualitative attribute exchanges for a quantitative one.

Arguably, by beginning *Capital* with a discussion of the commodity, seen as the microcosm of capitalist structures, Marx has also begun with capital's *form*. He does this not because he endorses formality, but because the evacuation/abstraction of the individual, the particular, the substantial—ultimately, the human—is precisely the crime of capital he wants to expose. Rhetorically speaking, he opens with an act/request to see something *as* something else—quality *as* quantity, labor *as* value, and so on—or to see something from two simultaneous points of view—quality *and* quantity, etc. In this important sense, then, form is also a principle of visibility and invites a type of *double vision* that has the potential to deliver a social critique.

Blackness has a very intimate relationship with the commodity form, one rooted in slavery, of course, but also one that survives in the way blackness has continued to circulate in popular and visual culture. So when we think about form in the Marxian sense—as a principle of visibility, as the appearance of something, both in the sense of its "coming into visibility" and in the sense of the way something *looks*—we are also thinking about blackness as that which makes the form of the commodity visible as such. It prompts us to not only attempt to more profoundly grasp what the commodification of blackness might mean but also ask: what kind of commodity is the one for which blackness acts as a principle of visibility? Or, said otherwise: What do we learn about the commodity form, when this form is black?

Color blindness as a visual culture problem

One of the main tensions intrinsic to the idea of color blindness is the fact that it is couched in the visual terms it is trying to disavow, yet it does not offer a critique of vision as a tool to identify racial difference, but instead assumes that one chooses to be "blind" to what one sees. By definition, then, color blindness is not only a social, formal, or legal problem but also a visual culture problem. As a result, color blindness can make a demand for equality only in a formal sense because, from the point of view of visual culture, it makes *no* sense.

Color blindness is a way to disavow the color line, which is also a visual culture problem. In fact, in visual culture, the assumed symmetry that sustains the ideology of color blindness does not obtain; while whiteness is a seemingly empty category and goes unmarked, as Richard Dyer was one of the first to observe, blackness is always notable and possesses a recognizable content.[5] Furthermore, the logic of segregation signs that during Jim Crow mapped the social body in binary terms—whereby the very fact that one water fountain is marked as "white" and another marked as "colored" is supposed to make them equal— was constantly contradicted at the level of material culture in the concrete differences in the ways the facilities were effectively designed. The water fountains do not compare equally, and actually loudly denounce how segregation is functional to the maintenance of inequality. This binarism does not occur at the social level either, since the social body is much more diverse than the separate-but-equal doctrine can accommodate. What facilities, for example, should have Asians occupied?

Here is the heart of the matter: by linking color blindness to formal equality, CRT also links visual culture to social equality. It does so with the awareness that visual culture cannot in itself resolve the problem of social equality. One reason for this is the specific way in which race is articulated in the visual field.

Race and the visual field

In *The Souls of Black Folk*, W. E. B. Du Bois predicted that the biggest issue of the twentieth century was going to be the question of race relations, which he described as the "color line." He also characterized the black subject as one affected by "double consciousness," or the effect of *seeing oneself through the eyes of another*. With concepts that express the visual construction of race—how race is most immediately, although not exclusively, apprehended as a marked difference in the visual field—Du Bois showed how Critical Race Theory is also always implicated with visual culture studies and how the color line is something that unfolds in visual culture, *as* visual culture.[6]

Du Bois prefaces his discussion of the idea of double consciousness with an episode from his youth, a "scene" where he suddenly discovered what it was to be defined by the gaze of another. One day at school, the young Du Bois attempted to exchange cards with a white girl, but she refused. "Then," he writes, "it dawned upon me with a certain suddenness that I was different from the others."[7] Frantz Fanon's *Black Skins, White Masks* contains a similar and even more dramatic scene: as he is traveling by train in France, the Martinican intellectual hears a child crying out to his mother, "Look, a Negro!" This is a seminal passage within Critical Race Theory because of how effectively it addresses the tension between the lived experience of race and its visual epistemology, that is, the fact that race is very much a way of knowing through vision. In both scenes, the subject realizes their difference because of how they are seen from the outside. In both cases, they experience a split between their self-fashioned image (i.e., the knowledge of themselves from the inside out) and the image that is being projected onto them. This second image imposes itself and alienates them, separates them and divides them, from the image of their own making. Du Bois describes this as an experience of "two-ness": the image of himself *as other* he cannot incorporate and, therefore, the sense of his racial identity as a manner of being split and doubled by definition. Fanon describes this same effect as a becoming aware of his body not just in the third person (i.e., seeing oneself from the outside, like an "object in the midst of other objects"), but "in triple," by feeling responsible for himself, his race, and his ancestors, and as the sensation of occupying too much space, taking up an excessive amount of room—two or three train seats, in fact.[8]

This traumatic encounter in the field of vision, this "color line" that is projected onto the subject who is identified or "hailed" as "black," is a "primal scene" that has been repeatedly compared to Jacques Lacan's theory of the mirror stage in psychoanalysis. Yet, here the subject is formed as *raced*—as racially marked—a form of alienation that both duplicates and challenges the process that Lacan described for the racially unmarked subject.

For Lacan, the mirror stage is where the child first encounters herself as an image. Having experienced herself only as a series of bodily fragments up to that point, the child encounters her "ideal" image in her reflection in the mirror and *misrecognizes* herself as whole (an entire body, a "full" person). The crucial point for Lacan is that this is a *mis*recognition and a form of alienation insofar as the child identifies with something that is not the self, but the outward image of the self.[9]

However, for someone who is already alienated within the social order, this moment has very different implications. Fanon notes how, when the colonized experiences the situation described by the Lacanian mirror stage, she does not register her own skin color; color does not factor into the ideal image she sees reflected in the mirror. Yet, her skin color is all that matters in the image that the colonized discovers once she is in the company of whites, and she will then be identified as "black." This "imago" (the image that exists between the seer and the seen) is produced socially, by a collective identification of the colonial subject with their skin color. Thus, another mirror reflection is superimposed to the originary one described by Lacan. Consequently, no ideal image, however illusory, is being made available to the child; she is given no sense of wholeness with which she can identify. The child is now suspended between two impossibilities: to recognize one's self or identify as other. Seen from the point of view of blackness, the Lacanian mirror functions in an inverted mode because it forces the black subject to become aware of her alienation from her own image, aware of the impossibility of existing as a whole, aware of her fundamental and hopeless fragmentation. The Black *begins* and *ends* violently fragmented.[10]

But there is another side to this process, which Du Bois described with the visual metaphor of the "veil." Du Bois says the Black is born under a "veil," or a coat of opacity that shrouds her into invisibility, a void or darkness created by cultural misrepresentations, and also the territory of the unknown, the mysterious, and the unclear. Because of the impenetrability it creates, the veil is made to bear the repressed fantasies of the master, acting as a screen of projection of collective misconceptions about the Black. Yet, for Du Bois, the veil is not simply a hindrance but also a resource. In fact, it is a two-sided screen: as it makes the Black opaque, it also affords her the possibility to look back while remaining unseen. By seeing through the veil, the observed becomes the observer: the Black sees not only the image of herself that the other has projected onto her, but also the (ideal) image that whiteness can construct for itself and, therefore, whiteness *as* an image. The veil, that is, institutes a second sight: the ability to *see oneself being seen*, to *see oneself seeing* (i.e., seeing the image of whiteness projected onto oneself *as* a screen), and to behold the entire *scene*. By seeing some version of herself directly in the mirror of the other's eyes, she is at all times the seen, the seer, and the scene. Similarly, by holding the black imago "in suspension"—just like he is suspended between the impossibility of finding an ideal reflection of the self and identifying with the image of the other that is projected onto him—Fanon ultimately conceptualizes blackness not as a visual property but rather as a visual *relation*; blackness is not something that preexists before this encounter but is rather its by-product.

Embodiment and epidermality

Black Skins, White Masks has been central to the understanding of the phenomenology of the black body, that is, the way in which the embodied subject experiences the encounter with this shattering image. In the phenomenological framework formulated by Maurice Merleau-Ponty, all knowledge is embodied because the body is the vehicle for consciousness of the world. "I am my body," claims the philosopher, and the body is the medium through which I am conscious of the world. The body is not an obstacle, as in the Cartesian tradition, but rather an indispensable tool.[11]

Prior to the encounter with the French child, Fanon describes knowledge of his own body from the inside out, through what he calls the "body schema." When moving in space, we are aware of our bodies' boundaries: how tall we are, and how wide. By the same token, for Merleau-Ponty, a cane becomes part of a blind man's body. This is the "body-schema." Yet, as he is hailed as a Negro, another schema overrides whatever knowledge the subject already had of himself. This is the "*epidermal* schema," a body-image that is entirely determined by one's skin color. As a consequence of the child's interpellation, Fanon has now become pure surface; he is turned inside out, and his identity, interiority, and personality are evacuated. There is no expectation of a thinking, intentional being behind epidermal blackness. "My subjectivity," writes Charles Johnson in his commentary on Fanon's passage, "is turned inside out like a shirtcuff."[12]

The "epidermality" of race describes the fact that race is found on the surface of the body and that skin color is always a cultural signifier, it always *means* something, and it always triggers a series of connotations that the subject cannot control. This all-surface subject is hypervisible (seen everywhere and from a distance) and hypervisual (the most visible thing, in fact, quintessential visibility). The epidermal signifier is also a fetish, acting as a cover for the unsightly discovery of racial difference, as well as a synecdoche, that is, a part for the whole. Consequently, in the fantasies of his white psychiatric patients, explains Fanon, the Negro is entirely eclipsed, and all that is left is the penis—indeed, for them, the Negro *is* a penis.

The visual is the terrain of an encounter not only between the other and the self but also of the self with itself. In the colonial situation, writes Fanon, the gaze of the other occupies the mind of the colonized, so that one does not have to experience a real encounter to feel the effects of the colonial gaze. As Johnson further writes, "It is *I* who perceive myself as 'stained.'" Epidermality and the visual *overdetermination* of the raced subject (what Fanon describes as the fact of being defined by his epidermal image *before*, *above*, and *beyond* anything else; in other words, to be already known in advance) are paradoxically also at the root of the social invisibility of Blacks. This is where blackness clearly emerges as an ontological problem insofar as it appears to have tremendous presence, substance, and power as a visual fact, but no footing, no positive and affirmative content on its own terms. While the white man is for the black man both the Other and the Master, the black man, Fanon observes, has "no ontological resistance" in the eyes of the white man.

The fact of blackness

In the 1967 English translation of *Black Skins, White Masks*, the chapter where Fanon unfolds the primal scene of racialization discussed so far—"Look, a Negro"—is titled

"The Fact of Blackness." Even though this was not a faithful translation of the original—which is more closely rendered by the 2008 translation by Richard Wilcox, who titles the same chapter "The Lived Experience of the Black Man"—it still vividly expressed how the black body is encountered in the visual field. The "fact" of blackness refers to the "givenness" of blackness in the field of vision.

To begin, the "factuality" of blackness in the field of vision is a consequence of the epidermalization of race, the fact that race is read off of the surface of the body, and that skin color is its primary signifier. In this sense, the factuality of blackness is strictly dependent on "surface readings," and, within an epistemological framework confident in the truth-value of vision, the fact of a body's blackness is the true signifier of its difference. Thus, the "fact of blackness" first and foremost expresses the overdetermination of the black body in the field of vision, or, to put it differently, the difficulty for the black body to be anything other than *black*. However, Fanon was careful to show that this *fact* is the product of the look of the other, who triggers the moment of racialization.

But what do we mean when we talk about "the black body?" Fanon emphasizes that even though we might think that blackness is visually undeniable, its "factuality" has to be constantly reinforced and repeated in order to be perceived as such. Visual culture studies shows that vision is always socially, culturally, and historically constructed, and that the social sphere is always visually constructed as well. Visual culture teaches the eye not only what to see but also how to see it. It is the idea of a natural vision and objective perception that constructs a body overdetermined by its blackness, which supersedes any other characterization of that body, such as gender, sexuality, class, status, and so on.

In another sense, the black body is the body seen from the outside; thus it is an abstraction from the individual body authorized by the latter's skin color. The blackness of the black body forms through the perception of a number of similarities across bodies. In this sense, the black body is its own image, not the body as *lived*. This image can be a shadow that stands over the body, or, when it is interiorized, a perceived stain lodged inside. Because it is an abstraction, the black body is also "epithetic" in the sense that it is *made black* the moment it is so named. In this way, the "black body" is constructed in the *present* moment of the interpellation that brings it into being, but it is also always connected to similar experiences of the same (black) body that have occurred in the *past*, which haunts it in the present.[13]

On another level, the "fact of blackness" refers to the insights Fanon offered on the psychic repercussions of the visuality of blackness. In the later 1980s and early 1990s, the essays of Homi Bhabha, Kobena Mercer, and Stuart Hall approached Fanon as a visual theorist of the colonial relation who emphasized the price that the interiorization of this relation demands from both the colonized and the colonizer. Leveraging Fanon's grounding in psychoanalysis, they highlighted both the "ambivalence" of colonial discourse and the ambivalence of their own subject position in relation to this discourse. Several concepts became available through this engagement. Stuart Hall's essay, "The After-Life of Frantz Fanon: Why Fanon? Why Now? Why *Black Skins, White Masks*?," emphasized the construction of black skin and the black body as a fetishized signifier of difference; it also expounded upon the "sexualization of the gaze," or the way the black body is both an object of fear and desire, and how tightly the black body is discursively constructed in order to bear the repressed fantasies of the colonizer.[14]

As a visual theorist, Fanon offered tools for thinking through strategies to "decolonize the mind" and reflect on the conditions for artistic freedom of self-expression. Thus, he became a major point of reference for a generation of minority artists and filmmakers who were reenvisioning their own places and roles within the visual arts. He offered a way to both understand and resist the "problem of the visual," or the limitations that are intrinsic to the attempt to represent oneself in a field that has historically been the primary way of marking the subject's inassimilable otherness. In other words, as Kobena Mercer asked, if the Black is always already visually fixated into a degraded signifier of difference, what artistic strategies are available to Blacks as image-*makers*? Because Fanon was so successfully able to explain how the "look" is implicated in the process of racialization and how powerfully the gaze of the other installs itself within the mind and perception of the colonized, the "look" also becomes the battleground for a more liberated self-definition. Black visual artists and filmmakers realize they have to "reenvision vision" in order to redefine the terms within which the black body is encountered in the field of vision.[15]

Formal equality in the field of vision

Given the (visual) fact of blackness, it is hard to imagine in what circumstances formal equality can be achieved in the field of vision. This is the issue at the core of *Plessy v. Ferguson* (1896), the Supreme Court decision that enshrined the doctrine of "separate but equal" and that instituted Jim Crow as a visual system of segregation. The case is therefore a defining moment for both CRT and visual culture studies. From its very conception, *Plessy* shows how segregation is an unmanageable visual culture project. The *Plessy* case, in fact, was the result of a strategic pass engineered by a committee of private citizens in New Orleans in order to challenge the constitutionality of the 1890 Louisiana State "Act to Promote the Comfort of Passengers," which had instituted separate train cars for blacks and whites. *Plessy* is also a decision that enshrines a fundamental split between formal and social equality, while also introducing the idea of a color-blind Constitution, which would then be evoked by Civil Rights legislation to support the law's indifference to race as an idea with a content.

Here are the salient facts. Homer Plessy was a light-skinned man who boarded a train and sat in a "white only" car before announcing to the conductor that he was a Negro. Because of his light complexion, Plessy had been purposely chosen as the legal test case in order to create a situation in which race was not clearly visually recognizable. Plessy's attorney, Albion Tourgée, adopted a multipronged strategy. His first goal was to render Jim Crow visually chaotic in order to argue against the right of the state to determine a person's race. If the burden of identifying race falls onto the beholder, this means that attribution of racial identity could be arbitrary and could easily result in the violation of the Fourteenth Amendment, which guarantees equal protection under the law.

On the issue of visual chaos, Justice Brown, who penned the Supreme Court majority decision, reestablished the validity of visual distinctions as indications of "natural" (and therefore biologically grounded) differences, "a distinction which is founded in the *color* of the two races and which must always exist so long as white men are distinguished from the other race by *color*."[16] Tourgée's second goal was to appeal to the Court's understanding of whiteness as property, arguing that the Louisiana statute violated Plessy's property rights in his own white appearance. His strategy was to call attention to the privileges associated with the possession of whiteness and advocate for the extension of the property whiteness to individuals who already possessed its corporeal appearance. This strategy backfired, and the majority argued that "passing" was not a legitimate ground for such a claim; the Court thereby protected the property right in whiteness and described Plessy's claim as an unauthorized appropriation. Ultimately, the *Plessy* case confirmed the mulatto as a site/sight of crisis—ironically one produced by the strategic conjunction of "property" and "reproduction" in plantation economy, that is, the fact that mulattoes were the result of the systemic rape of slave women, and, given that children would follow the legal status of the mother, they were also a way to increase capital for the slave owners—and therefore also as a threat to the exclusivity of the property whiteness.

Finally, Tourgée argued for the inequality of segregation by showing how *formal equality* is intrinsically asymmetrical.

For him, the fact that black nurses could accompany whites in the white-only car, as part of the so-called nurse exception, indicated that the rationale for this separation was to protect the comfort of whites, not blacks. In order to further press this issue, he deployed a "counterfactual" to test the Court's imagination of a reversed scenario: he asked members of the Court to imagine themselves in Plessy's shoes in order to understand his property claim to some of the privileges of whiteness. What would happen, Tourgée asked, if the Justices had woken up one morning with black skin and curly hair and they had been asked to move to the colored car?

Because of its implied symmetry, the counterfactual logic underlies both the doctrine of separate-but-equal and the philosophy of color blindness.[17] The counterfactual is a narrative form that seeks to identify material causes by producing a mirror-like, imaginary, and inverted equivalent of the actual world. It is a thought experiment that depends on the ability to imagine the tables turned. As such, it is also subjected to the limitations of the imagination and, sometimes, as happened to the Court in *Plessy*, it might fail to envision an alternative to the existing world. In fact, by arguing that segregation applied equally to all races, Justice Brown established a formalist theory of symmetrical equality that he could advance because he distinguished between political and social equality. For him, social equality was beyond the scope of constitutional protection and incompatible with biologically based natural differences between the races. Finally, he argued that the "feeling of inferiority" that the black race might experience as a consequence of segregation is beyond the scope of the law. He thus produced a double injury: not only was Plessy's grievance left unattended but also the very experience of discrimination was preemptively discarded.

Plessy is also a pivotal case in establishing the idea that the Constitution is color-blind. This was the claim that Justice Harlan made in his dissenting opinion, wherein he argued against the idea of the symmetry of the Jim Crow system and for the recognition of inequality and racial injury. He wrote, "Our constitution is color-blind, and neither knows nor tolerates classes among citizens."[18] Yet, as Neil Gotanda has shown, Civil Rights legislation took this claim as a statement of fact—that the Constitution *is* in fact color-blind—to argue against taking race into any kind of consideration. The outcome, once again, is the reliance on formal equality.

The *Plessy* case also occupies a special place in the history of American privacy law. Within the rhetoric of "possessive individualism," whereby a person has property rights over her identity, the self-possessed subject is granted a private sphere, which is part of her identity because it is part of her property. Privacy protects that which it constructs—for example, the right to an "inside" as a space of individual sovereignty that can be mobilized to perform acts of exclusion. Privacy is produced by property, property is an attribute of whiteness, and whiteness can institute virtually any sphere as "private" (and therefore exclusive). Ultimately whiteness appears in the law as the reification of expectations of white privilege; whiteness gives a claim to racial purity, a way to construct and protect one's privacy, and the absolute right to exclude.[19]

Plessy in visual culture studies

The *Plessy* case consolidates an economy of legibility that regulates bodies in the social sphere on the basis of their skin color. Within it, the passing body always brings a crisis of representation because it possesses visual qualities that betray its biological origin, as well as the legal construction of that supposedly natural origin. Yet, even though Tourgée's argument did not hold, he succeeded in exposing the "hallucinatory character" of Jim Crow laws.[20]

In part, this is a confirmation of what, building on Michel Foucault, Robyn Wiegman has called the "racial panopticon." The panopticon designates the system of surveillance first imagined at the end of the eighteenth century by Jeremy Bentham's model for a prison in which inmates are disciplined by their awareness of being subjected at all times to the surveillance of a gaze they cannot see. Because of the impossibility for the inmates to know whether they are being watched at any specific time, this gaze is eventually interiorized. For Wiegman, the very visibility of skin color institutes a similar form of surveillance, and thus the threat of being disciplined, because one is always being seen.[21] For example, if, in the Jim Crow regime, a dark-skinned individual were to attempt to drink from a water fountain reserved for whites, this act of transgression would be immediately evident to anybody around her.

In the *Plessy* case, Tourgée argued that Jim Crow reconstructs the essence of slavery with the difference that now, because of the panoptic logic of visibility of skin color, one is no longer the property of a single owner but of the whole white race. This racial panopticon had been ratified by law even earlier with the Fugitive Slave Law of 1850, which compelled all free citizens to act as proxies of the master's gaze. It therefore wrote into law the informal system that had already instituted "whiteness" as an attribute (a property) that implied the presumption of freedom, while blackness implied the presumption of captivity. It also extended the speculation in slaves to all US states and the commodity form to all blacks, regardless of their free or non-free status.

At the same time, *Plessy* foregrounds how the law supports a visual logic of binary oppositions instituted in the name of an implied "symmetry" in the condition of the two races. This same logic also governs the aesthetics and rhetoric of segregation signs, which function on the assumption of formal equality. As visual culture scholar Elizabeth Abel argues, the signs "colored" and "white" institute a "racial symbolic order" when placed on a bathroom door or above a water fountain. Similar to Lacan's Symbolic order, that is, the language or system of signifiers and codes that structures the norms of society and our place in it, in segregation signs, reading and racialization are mutually constitutive, given how language competence and literacy are required to identify one's position within this order. Language very directly regulates one's position in the social space. Other conditions being equal, reading is used to identify the bathroom one is supposed to use.

Segregation demands self-disclosure, insofar as one has to willingly take up a predetermined raced and gendered position. At the same time, every act of acquiescence to the laws of segregation unwillingly reinforces its mode of signification.[22] Beginning in the 1940s, photographs of segregated facilities, such as bathrooms and water fountains, taken by northern photographers shocked by the blatant inscription of race in the landscape, disclose the extent to which the bathrooms or water fountains do not exchange in equal terms because of their location and appearance. Thus, it is through the visual culture of segregation signs that the intrinsic inequality of segregation becomes fully visible, along with the hallucinatory character of the visual culture of segregation that is supposed to maintain equivalences where there are none.

Plessy also offers a meeting point between visual culture studies and the logic of capitalism because passing partakes of the logic of the commodity form; passing is a site of exchange on the basis of a perceived likeness. From the point of view of appearances, in fact, skin tone *exchanges for* racial identity, visual appearance for essence, and the legibility of appearance for its truth.

Ultimately, the parameters for *formality*, *likeness*, and *exchange* that the Plessy case consolidates have a much broader cultural life than the legal sphere. A few years after the *Plessy* decision, in fact, the infant medium of the cinema expresses, through an interracial narrative about train travel, a counterfactual imagination that supports the illusion of the separate-but-equal. It does so by resorting to a black screen.

Screen blackness as scene of exchange

In *What Happened in the Tunnel* (Edwin Porter, 1903), a three-minute film set on a train car just a few years after the *Plessy* decision, a white woman traveling with her black maid is the target of a white man's sexual advances. Suddenly, the train enters a tunnel, the screen fades to black and, as the screen image reappears *on the other side* of the tunnel, the man finds himself kissing the maid instead, who, taking advantage of the filmic and profilmic darkness, has exchanged places with her mistress.

This fade to black has fascinated many early film scholars because of the way it marks a rich exchange between a variety of disparate things: between the two women, who have traded places in the train; between potential sexual partners (the joke of the film is that the man is shocked to discover he has kissed the maid instead of the white woman); between screen blackness and a void (the tunnel); between screen blackness and the maid's epidermal blackness; and between temporal and spatial ellipsis and a few seconds of cinematic emptiness.

The film has been read in the context of other trick films, of the cinema of attractions, or again as partaking of a "free-floating visuality" that creates the space for this joke of substitution. It is discussed as an example of the transition toward narrative cinema, whereby films with two shots become capable of telling a story rather than simply showing a situation. And it was made at a time when audiences were beginning to wonder about what happens in between cuts. This screen blackness has also been analyzed as a signifier of movement into the tunnel and, more importantly, of lateral movement inside the frame, which renders the crossing of racial boundaries as a movement through space.[23] Finally, the film's title promises a total vision but fails to provide it; we can't see in the darkness, and the film can't show the inside of (an interracial) kiss. Ushering in a moment of suspension, the screen blackness conveys an important entanglement—a kiss that is a substitute for intercourse. Ultimately, the "switcheroo" is a way to process a fantasy of introjection of the other, whereby screen blackness also functions as a form of interpenetration and, therefore, as a site of racial melancholia as well.

This screen blackness is also ripe for a close interrogation of ideas of "formal equality" mobilized in the "separate-but-equal" doctrine and considerations of how the blackness of the on-screen body "authorizes," so to speak, the "switch" that constitutes the joke of the film. In these multiple substitutions, in fact, we can also recognize the logic of the counterfactual, insofar as the film stages a mirror-like inverted scenario where the tables are indeed turned. While the screen blackness delivers a scene of counterfactual exchange, it stages the conflation between equality and equation that one finds broadly represented in the binary logic of segregation signs. Yet, what is disclosed here is not the prospect of *equality*—if the man had been pleased with the switch, there would be no punch line to the joke—but rather simply a process of *equation* (between screen blackness and the racial blackness of the substituted diegetic body). Blackness, in its broader sense, performs as both a *scene* and a *signifier* of *exchange*, while the film instructs its spectators to comprehend an emerging social logic of segregation and its attendant visual culture.

Two fundamental tensions remain. The first is between movement and fixation. Plessy successfully passes, but the *Plessy* case stills his movement, fixating and codifying the understanding of race as a visual epistemology. *What Happened in the Tunnel*, instead, sets this pass back in motion by leveraging its most extreme visual manifestation, chromatic blackness, as signifier of a hole one passes through (i.e., the tunnel). Second, there remains a tension between passing as a movement from subject to subject (black passing for white, in Plessy's case), and subject to object (in the maid's case, a subject exchanging for an abstraction or an emptiness, a hole).

Formal equality and aesthetics of commodification

Passing partakes of the logic of the commodity form to the extent that it is grounded on the "likeness" necessary for two qualitatively different things to exchange with one another. This is how the commodity form both presupposes and stages formal equality. John Stahl's *Imitation of Life* (1934) has been amply discussed in this context.[24] The film has a passing character—Peola, the light-skinned daughter of the maid Delilah—and an obviously black one, the mother. In this first cinematic adaptation of the Fannie Hurst novel (the second one is Douglas Sirk's 1959 film by the same title), Peola is played by Freddie Washington, who is also a light-skinned biracial woman. In the context of the film, it is clear that Peola's white appearance gives her mobility and exchangeability in a white world; to the extent that she is visually equivalent to whites, she can also be equal to them.

Peola creates a rhetorical crisis insofar as her visual appearance disrupts Hollywood's artificially enforced continuity between color, skin, race, and blood. The Production Code Administration's censorship of the script on the basis of the violation of the miscegenation clause, in fact, makes constant reference to both visual and biological markers of Peola's identity—for example, "the white child of a Negro mother with colored blood"—and to the fact that she looks one way but is really something else.[25] Furthermore, Freddie Washington's own appearance brings a representational and aesthetic crisis to the heart of photographic knowledge; it challenges photography's supposed transparency because it constantly frustrates the viewer about the possibility of seeing who she "really" is.

To contain Peola's ability to pass, the film deploys a series of strategies to ensure that blackness exchanges with things and not people, and, in the process, it stages another passage: from the person to the commodity object. Delilah's employer and "friend" Bea decides to open a store on the Atlantic City boardwalk to sell Delilah's pancakes. As she is discussing the aesthetics of a sign she would like to have put on her storefront, she asks Delilah to strike a pose: head tilted slightly upward and in profile, gaze high into the distance, with a broad smile. Delilah complies, and Bea fixates this pose with her reaction: "that's it!" Delilah remains frozen in this pose well after Bea has stopped describing the sign, a fact that the film handles as a humorous moment. Bea is projecting what she finally recognizes—that is, the image of a black woman that consumer culture has fostered, in other words, not Delilah, but "Aunt Delilah"—and the film invites the spectator to do the same. Later, a montage sequence shows the growing success of her employer, Bea, through the increasing magnification, stylization, and abstraction of Delilah's face over an array of commodities. Delilah is the live model for the store sign; her face features on the pancake box and is then outlined in a gigantic neon sign overlooking Times Square. The film visualizes her "passage" into commodity culture as a principle of *iconic* equivalence between the black subject and commodity objects, and as a system of *resemblances* among these signs and between them and their model.

During the rise of mass consumption after the turn of the century, the image of the racial other featured prominently on brands or trademarks and thus performed as a sort of "second skin" that commodity objects assume in order to interface with their consumers. It offered a way for white citizens to strengthen their own disembodiment as citizens while having quotidian intimate contacts with vestiges of the overembodied other. Delilah's blackness provides a similar second skin, in the sense that her trademark is an outgrowth of an already marked body that offers an experience of corporeality through consumption; in the process, she also gives a human face to the commodity fetish.[26]

In a Marxian sense, commodity fetishism is associated with two things: one is the invisibility of labor, which does not leave a trace on the commodity object, and the other is the animism that derives from this fact. Seen through its fetish, the commodity does not appear man-made but rather is born fully formed, so to speak, and moving—in fact "dancing"— of its own volition.[27] The slave offers a prototype for this convergence of self-origination and liveness. As the character Topsy claims, in Margaret Stowe's *Uncle Tom's Cabin*, "*I 'spect I grow'd. Don't think nobody never made me.*" Topsy is the prototypical black child who is always compulsively moving, performing so vividly that, as commentators at the time tirelessly remarked, she appeared to almost "leap" out of the page. The dancing, gesturing, emoting commodity calls attention to how the sensuousness of the object's aesthetic properties increase the experience and attraction of the commodity fetish. This heightened motility is paired with her inability to account for her origin as if she was born complete, just like the commodity fetish conceals the traces of the labor that accounts for the commodity's existence.

The counterpart to commodity fetishism is the advertising aesthetics of "capitalist realism," that is, the imagination/materialization of a way of experiencing things that supports the material and social relations of capitalism. Fully self-contained and self-referential, capitalist realism does not make truth claims about the world; rather, it is entirely self-directed and self-sufficient and therefore occupies its own plane of reality. Its only goal is to provide an interface to enable capitalist social relations to romance themselves.[28] The advertising image is the mere vehicle, the temporary embodiment necessary for this romance to take place so that, when Delilah's face multiples across commodity culture, she becomes a sensuous medium for capitalism to say "I love you" to itself.

How race is made: Race and the human sensorium

In order to induce the sense that there is something unaccounted for in some of the categories employed, I pitted the expected formal equality of segregation against the visual chaos and hallucinatory nature of the visual culture of segregation, while also discussing the representational crisis of the passing body in relation to the sensuousness of the surface of the commodity object. Race is visual, and there is no denying that, but it is also material, as this discussion of commodity aesthetics indicates. Race engages the entire human sensorium so that the disavowal presupposed by the color line is ultimately not simply a denial of the truth-value of sight but also of the much more complex and deeper sensorial construction of race. If we remain with *Plessy* a bit longer, some of this will come into focus.

The "great age of passing" was from 1880 to 1925. Railroads introduced a new mobility for people, whereby it was no longer possible to know one's genealogy and, therefore, one's racial identity. Plessy's pass called attention to the fallacy of knowledge by sight, or the idea that one will be able to accurately read identity from appearance. At the same time, it threatened the confidence that white Southerners had in their ability to identify race. For them, race was never just simply a visual fact. In *How Race Is Made*, Mark Smith outlines instead a history of how all the senses were enlisted to cooperate in the construction of race. The senses facilitated the experience of *feeling* race, strengthening the idea that race is, in fact, *real* and tangible, and thus making people comfortable with the racial worlds they had created.[29]

In turn, sense experience is not given, but *made*, and the senses are *made to make sense* in particular historically, culturally, and socially inflected ways. Smith outlines various phases, patterns, and forms of regulation of the human sensorium in different moments of US racial history to show the shifting ways in which whites gave a sensorial foundation to blackness. For example, as much as the logic of segregation insisted on symmetrical binarisms and the rigidity of the color line, Southerners produced a complicated and erratic sensorial landscape in which rules of discrimination were capriciously enforced, as well as conveniently suspended, to whites' advantage. After all, labor relations still demanded that blacks engage in a variety of types of close contacts with whites, such as cooking and nursing. Far from weakening the color line, these exceptions would effectively augment the authority of whites.

In traditional pictorial aesthetics, the idea of the "color line" is an oxymoron because color is supposed to be a secondary feature to the line. The line is considered the "primary quality" because it is that which bestows clear boundaries to objects, which are then "filled in" with color. The line is objective—it belongs to the object—while color is subjective and lives in the eyes of the beholder. The idea of the color line reverses the traditional relationship between "content" and "form." With regard to race, it is as if color has been objectified and *has become* a tangible substance that produces its own boundary—indeed, a line. Furthermore, in racial terms it is color, not the line, which acts as a principle of intelligibility.

Smith offers the possibility of thinking about the color line as a form of organization of the human sensorium supposed to corroborate, or sometimes supplement or substitute for, the visual construction of race. He discovers an imagery of black density forming in response to the illegibility of skin color—for example, the presumption of a distinctive "black odor," or the idea that black skin is insensitive to pain and suitable for beating. During segregation, Southerners even reported specific corporeal reactions in response to their sudden detection of blackness, like a twitch on the shoulder. What these (only apparently involuntary) reactions indicate instead is the trained organization of one's sensorium in the pursuit of blackness as an identifiable and tangible *thing*. They show how *race is* effectively *made*—built and put together—through a sensorial effort that will become important for the way *Bamboozled* constructs blackness on-screen: by means of a complex sensorial "thickness," or as an experience of "density" upon coming into contact with blackness.

If one were to undertake the sensorial history that Smith pursues, one would become sensitive to the many ways in which the black body is felt to exceed its boundaries: smell is one way, sound is another. These attributes of the apparently constitutively excessive and "incontinent" racial body are in fact primitivist attributions; the incontinence is considered a property of the primitive *body*, while it is in fact a construct of primitive *thinking* about this body. Sometimes, this quality of the raced body has been described after Julia Kristeva, through the concept of *abjection*, which indicates "aspects of oneself that one cannot be rid of, that seem, but are not quite, alienable . . . what cannot be subject or object to you."[30] In biological terms, the abject is what demands expulsion yet cannot be successfully expelled; it is a way to describe the uncomfortable border of the body; what sits at the boundary between me and not me and threatens that very boundary— for example, excrement or the corpse. In broader cultural terms, it is a way to draw a boundary between the human and the nonhuman; with a greater figural import, abjection indicates debasement, degradation, and defilement, and, at the same time, its dangerous seduction. The abject might describe an excess of materiality, flesh or filth and "too much" body at times associated with the racial grotesque or racist kitsch, which in turn can be leveraged to provide a critique of the boundaries of corporeal integrity, propriety, or humanity from which one is being abjected.

"I secreted a race"

The Fanonian primal scene describes race *in the making*. In addition to theorizing blackness as a visual relation rather than a property of his body, Fanon emphasizes how his blackness is the outcome of cooperation between his sensorium and the child's. He describes a sense of hemorrhaging and a feeling of nausea as consequences of the child's interpellation. Importantly, he does not voice only the perspective of the "race-*maker*" but also that of the subject who is being racialized, the subject to whom race is *done*. His description emphasizes the epithetic nature of blackness as something that *happens* to the body that is hailed as black. And, it happens *in* the body as a series of sensorial experiences to which the subject is attempting to give coherence. Below is a passage that shows race being made. It follows the child's interpellation, "Look, a Negro":

My body was returned to me spread-eagled, disjointed, redone, draped in mourning on this white winter's day. The Negro is an animal, the Negro is bad, the Negro is wicked, the Negro is ugly; look, a Negro; the Negro is trembling, the Negro is trembling because he's cold, the small boy is trembling because he's afraid of the Negro, the Negro is trembling with cold, the cold that chills the bones, the lovely little boy is trembling because he thinks the Negro is trembling with race, the little white boy runs to his mother's arms: "*Maman*, the Negro's going to eat me."[31]

This oscillatory structure—between the Negro as the object of the child's gaze, the Negro as a culturally fashioned object, the Negro as experienced by Fanon in the third person, and then back to the beholder of the gaze—is an example of how Fanon redirects the splitting force of racist interpellation that makes him aware of his body in the triple person. By doing so, it constructs blackness as a switch point between the seen, the seer, and the scene. But, just as importantly, it describes the moment of racialization as a series of bodily reactions, some of which belong to Fanon and others to the child who is performing the primitivist act. Yet, they mingle in Fanon's prose, especially with reference to the fact that both the child and Fanon are trembling (one with fear and the other "*with race*") so that Fanon is forced to conclude, "I *secreted* a race."[32]

This striking imagery of "secretion" is less rare than one might imagine (and features prominently in *Bamboozled*). It suggests Fanon's awareness of how his sensorium is forced to cooperate in the *making* of race for the observer. He has unwillingly *produced* the color line that sets him apart. Charles Johnson has also called attention to physiological reactions occurring in the moment of interpellation: his pulse and adrenaline increase, his skin becomes moist, he has the feeling that his consciousness has disappeared under a thick corporeality and the sense of being "slumberous, torpid matter." He diagnoses the very process whereby the optical overflows its own boundaries and spills into a more complex sensoriality by describing epidermalization as something that "spreads throughout the body like an odor, like an echoing sound."[33]

It is not surprising that phenomenological approaches to the lived experience of the black body would provide "thick" descriptions such as these, but here there is a specific commitment to producing an effect of *density* as a reaction to a missing ontological ground—the fact that the Black "has no *ontological resistance* in the eyes of the white man." Thickness and density, in this context, are ways to push back and put up some kind of resistance by asserting the presence of a living body that *feels* what this process of racialization is doing to it.

"I dream I am jumping, swimming, running, and climbing"

One of the things that the racialized body feels is the desire to explode. In Frantz Fanon's *The Wretched of the Earth*, there is a recurring image of the colonized in a perpetual state of muscle contraction. "Hemmed in" by a repressive Manichean colonial regime, the native has recurring dreams of muscular prowess and aggressive vitality. "I dream I am jumping, swimming, running, and climbing," writes Fanon, "I dream I burst out laughing, I am leaping across a river or I am followed by a flood of motorcars which never catch up with me."[34] These tense muscles describe both how the colonial regime is lived at the level of the body and a situation of possible eruption and explosion. The living body subjected to racialization needs to reassert its corporeal coherence, its presence in space, and its existence in time.

However, space and time are asymmetrical categories from the point of view of race. James Snead has argued that, within Enlightenment philosophy (and certainly with Hegel), the Black has been conceptualized as occupying space, but not living in historical time. Time belongs to the European, who has agency over history, while the native is "internal to time" in the sense that she is imagined as always-already-there (in Africa, that is) and unable to evolve.[35] In other words, the temporal structure of the colonial regime does not afford a present time within which the colonized can, in fact, *be* or even act out. The colonized exists in between the anticipation of this explosion, which is attributed to the native's inability to control herself, and the very event of colonialism or racism, which has created the need to explode in the first place. Kara Keeling observes how Fanon describes the black subject as living in a perpetual "interval," without direct access to the present moment, unless it is *through* or *as* affect. The Black accesses the present only via his/her "*feeling*: how does it feel to be Black?"[36]

Eating the other

Mark Smith makes clear that the strength of the color line depended equally on its enforcement and its transgression. bell hooks has described this sort of dynamic as "eating the other." She deploys a primitivist metaphor of incorporation normally projected onto the other, to indicate the desire to possess the other and to be somehow changed by the encounter. Yet, unless the other is clearly identifiable as such, this incorporation does not have any erotic interest; difference needs to be affirmed before it can be erotically cancelled out.[37]

There are several tropes of similarly ambivalent incorporation animating a variety of aesthetic concepts encountered thus far—for example, the aesthetic interface of the commodity in the trademark or logo. The trademark traffics in fantasies of incorporation such that ownership of a specific product sometimes feels like eating a bit of the other. As a corporeal supplement of the commodity object, it holds the promise of a bodily contact and intimacy. But, even in our discussion of screen blackness as a scene of exchange in *What Happened in the Tunnel*, we have found several forms of incorporation enacted as a series of substitutions: at a first diegetic level, screen blackness in the film substitutes for a kiss, which substitutes for intercourse; on another level, the body of a black woman substitutes for the body of a white woman; and a few seconds of screen time spent in complete blackness substitute for, as well as incorporate, all of the previously unimaginable substitutions mentioned above.

As bell hooks' choice of the term "eating" indicates, a lot of the ambivalence of fantasies of incorporation is conveniently projected onto the object that one wants to incorporate; it is the other that is accused of cannibalism, voraciousness, and a general inability to contain their appetite. This clearly appears in the long history of disparaging associations of blacks with food, both as objects of consumption and as subjects unable to control their eating impulses. This ambivalence conveniently maintains a reversibility between the incorporating and the incorporated.

Racial melancholia

Yet, there is another type of incorporation that is performed by the subject of injury. Much discourse about stereotypes is couched within the notion that, if interiorized, negative images will produce self-hatred. This idea was at the root of the sociological experiments that Kenneth and Mamie Clark conducted with schoolchildren and dolls—experiments that were used in the groundbreaking Supreme Court decision *Brown v. Board of Education* (1954), which reversed the doctrine of separate but equal. The Clarks observed African American children consistently choosing white dolls over black ones and were able to argue that the effect of segregation is to create a feeling of inferiority.

In political theory, *Brown v. Board of Education* is sometimes considered as marking a shift from the idea of the country as "one" to the idea of the country as something that has to *become* a "whole."[38] Yet, because of its corporeal connotations, the very concept of "assimilation" depends on ideas of profound, even molecular, forms of incorporation and absorption and therefore is an idea fraught with ambivalence that can be seen as profoundly melancholic.

Furthermore, as Kobena Mercer elaborates in relation to the Fanonian primal scene, seeing oneself reflected in the other's reaction can complicate one's access to self-representation to the point that the image that the other projects—a negative stereotype, for example—becomes a sort of "internal foreign object" around which self-perception is always "alienated" by the way in which one is "perceived by others as *the* Other."[39]

In *The Melancholy of Race*, Anne Cheng analyzes the relationship between the racial other and the national drama of assimilation in terms of racial melancholia.[40] Taking inspiration in part from Toni Morrison's identification of the American literary canon as a melancholic corpus, Cheng shows how this melancholia can be richly described through a Freudian lens. Unlike mourning, where the mourner becomes capable of letting go of the lost object, melancholia is a pathological response to loss whereby one becomes attached to it; loss becomes interminable because the lost object cannot be replaced. Thus, the object lingers and is eventually "introjected" and incorporated. This is necessary for the melancholic subject because introjection provides a fiction of possession that denies the initial loss. But, because it is a form of possession more intimate than any material relation, this cannibalistic incorporation is also the only sure way the lost object will never return and the melancholic relation will continue; the melancholic subject will continue to "feed off" of the lost object. In this sense, melancholia does not so much express a loss so much as a voracious and insatiable appetite. The melancholic is not so because she has lost something, but because she has incorporated something that she now loathes.

Both the attachment to, and the dynamics of, assimilation in American culture are fundamentally melancholic in the sense of expressing an attachment to an "other" that is both inside and outside, introjected and ejected, desired and reviled, disposable, but necessary as well. Cheng's analysis of the structure of assimilation also focuses on the subjectivity of the *melancholic object*, that is, the way in which this melancholia affects the other, who is both rejected and incorporated, reviled and desired. The Prologue for Ralph Ellison's *Invisible Man* offers an illustration of the importance of this question and of the complexity of the melancholic relation. It begins with a famous declaration of invisibility ("I am an invisible man") that introduces the visual concept sustaining the book: the Black is invisible, that is, consciously constructed as an absence, because of her hypervisibility.[41] Yet, the melancholic relation is triggered by the fact that the protagonist's bumping into a white man is what prompts the realization of his invisibility. Angered, he interprets the white man's oversight as the product of the construction of his presence as a negative space of invisibility. Yet, upon closer reading, one notices that it is the invisible man who has bumped into the white man, and, therefore, there is ambiguity about who is really invisible and who is responsible for bumping into whom. Ultimately, the invisible man's paranoia about his invisibility is the outcome of an introjection of his own rejection; the invisible man is both a melancholic object and a melancholic subject, both the lost object and the losing subject. He is invisible because he has assimilated his own inassimilability.

The idea of racial melancholia can shed more light not only on the complexity of assimilation but also on the codependence between whiteness and its others. Ultimately, however, it is the object of this melancholia (i.e., the body considered "primitive") who is made to somatize (and therefore embody) the fear of contagion she is apparently causing.

Thinking about assimilation as the national drama of wholeness through the idea of melancholia affords a lens to reflect more minutely about moments and situations of racial entanglement and to realize how quotidian and, yet, abusive they are. Thus, here is the problem: racism is intimate, but, conversely, intimacy does not guarantee freedom from racism. Intimacy cannot resolve the question of whether the desire for another is an appetite or a form of generosity.[42] Indeed, scholarship that has focused on practices, fantasies, and failures of "amalgamation" in the context of conversations about a post-racial society has done so not with a sense of accomplishment but rather with the idea that, in these very same quotidian acts, we still find the afterlife of slavery. Too many domestic or everyday scenes of subjection get rewritten as scenes of intimacy and, therefore, of potential freedom, whereas they are forms of horrors lubricated by the desires that attend to racial melancholia.[43]

How race is done: Racial performativity

The idea of performativity has been central to the conceptualization of racial identity as something that is not fixed or pre-given but rather produced and reproduced through repetition of ritualized acts and gestures. Commonsensically, one can "talk black" or "dress white," and the performativity of race is implied in each one of these statements. Performativity emphasizes how racial identity is not simply something one *has* but rather something that one *does*, a process that unfolds through a series of repeated acts—a script, a corporeal style, but also a strategy for cultural survival grounded on a distinctive history of black expressive culture. Whether identified through the phenomenon of passing, or mimicry, or cross-racial identification and appropriation, racial performativity works against the idea of authenticity and essentialism, and focuses instead on how race is constantly made and remade through action, that is, by *doing it*.

The black body comes with an expectation of integrity: that you'd get what you see. Performativity can therefore be described as the "doing" located in the space between the body and its image; it indicates that something can be done about this expected coincidence between image and identity. In other words, the idea of the performativity of race emphasizes that, even though the black body is constructed as a visual problem, it can also trouble the vision that constructs it so.

The preacher's sermon in the prologue of *Invisible Man*, "Black is, black ain't," is central to this idea of performativity.

There, Ellison plays with the instability of the signifier "black" in order to show blackness as a series of constant beginnings; as something that is never accomplished, never secured, never fixed; as a process and a practice.[44] Language-use is a recognized sphere of performance, and, in *The Signifying Monkey*, Henry Louis Gates locates the blackness of a cultural expression in the ability to insert difference at the level of the signifier. This is a difference in use, direction, and deployment of language, which he describes as signifyin(g) in order to typographically visualize the different intonation that blackness might bring to a cultural utterance.[45] It is also an implicit recognition that race is, in many ways, just a trope.

Yet, race scholars are careful to emphasize that the visual fact of blackness at times overrides any power of invention and creation that racial performativity might otherwise afford. At the same time, they resist "the endemic relationship between performance and blackness," that is, the expectation that the Black should always perform, act, entertain, or move (like Topsy), or the idea of a natural talent associated with certain types of movements, such as proficiency in sports or propensity for rhythm.[46]

Blackness as thing

CRT scholarship has shown how whiteness is the product of a process of reification, enacted by US law, of expectations of white privilege. Broadly conceived, reification is the process identified by Marx whereby people appear as things, or relationships between people become things; it is the "becoming-material" of social relations. The fact that, up until 1957, one could still sue for being erroneously called "black" shows that the law protects the property whiteness and effectively recognizes that "it's a *thing*" (colloquially speaking). This process of reification is what produces "whiteness" out of "white people" and, conversely, can make "white people" out of ethnic groups that at one time did not have any property rights in whiteness.

Whiteness is a property, but of a special kind. Unlike most properties, whiteness is not alienable; it cannot be given up or traded. In this sense, it is more of a personal asset like an educational degree, which cannot be lost or shared, even as a consequence of a divorce. Yet, like other properties, whiteness does imply the right of *use* and *enjoyment*, and, in this sense, it is a usable property. Whiteness is a resource, and it gives the right to exclude. Whiteness is born out of the delimitation of privilege for the exclusive use of "white" people, which tells us that just like race has to be *made*, white people have to be made as well. One of the paradoxes of whiteness is that it implicitly acts as the universal norm but is instead a form of particularity.

On the side of blackness, however, matters are quite different. Blackness, too, is a thing, but of a very different kind. In the context of slavery, blackness is the mark of the property-status of the slave, but the slave is also straightforwardly described as a *thing*—sometimes labeled *negotium* (which emphasizes the property aspect) or *instrumentum vocale* (speaking *tool*). Scholarship focused on transatlantic slavery and its literature—both abolitionist and slave narratives—has made clear how the slave also initially perceives herself as one thing among other things, and how the slave has to learn her difference from these things in order to become the speaking subject who eventually narrates her own life story. Even Fanon opens his chapter on "The Lived Experience of the Black Man" by lamenting his coming into the world with a thirst to "attain" to its source and meaning, but instead finding himself to be "an object among other objects."[47]

Recently, blackness and whiteness have been conceptualized as types of *assemblages* with things to describe the way interactions with objects can produce racially defined subject positions. This is what Robin Bernstein has called a "dancing with things," that is, the way interactions with things are codified in repertoires of gestures consolidated along racial lines. Things can script the movement of humans around them and carry the memory of their past usage. Cast-iron piggy banks, like the Jolly Nigger bank featured in *Bamboozled*, were still relished as pedagogical tools in the 1930s and 1940s, insofar as children could learn the values of thrift in their repeated interactions with them. Abecedaries with racist illustrations—E.W. Kemble's 1898 *A Coon Alphabet*, for example—would teach not only literacy but also the values of white supremacy with each turn of the page. Thus, racial identity as well as racial hierarchy can be produced as an assemblage with the object.[48]

There are coerced assemblages—the slave and his/her shackles, for example—and assemblages that are sought after so that they can ignite a performance of race or of supremacy—for example, the interaction with "black" objects as described above, or the assemblage constructed among burnt cork, white gloves, red lipstick, and so on, creating the minstrel as a performance of blackness. Bernstein found a remarkable example of racial assemblage in the photograph of a woman posing with a larger-than-life wooden caricature of an African American eating watermelon at the Hotel Exposition in New York City's Grand Central Palace, circa 1930. The way the woman wrapped herself around the cutout and interacted with it, mimicking its broad smile and touching its hand with hers, became a performance of blackness only functional to the construction of her own whiteness. The woman in the picture—Helen Hernandez, a Hispanic in today's parlance, whose whiteness at the time was just beginning to be legally recognized—played with a recognizable thing, the caricature itself, in order to separate herself from its thingness; she played with a piece of property in order to show that she was not one. Bernstein reads this as a performance of *possessive individualism*, whereby the woman's interaction with the statue is a way for her to assert that she has full property over herself.

Interactions with objects are profoundly influenced by a person's orientation in the world. When Frantz Fanon describes the experience of his body prior to the child's interpellation, he does so through the language of phenomenology: "I know that if I want to smoke, I shall have to stretch out my right arm and grab the pack of cigarettes lying at the other end the table. As for the matches, they are in the left drawer." He insists, "And I make all these moves, not out of habit, but by implicit knowledge."[49] The body Fanon describes is "ready for action," and its gesture (smoking, in this case) is the effect of his orientation in the world.

Because orientation is the point from which the world unfolds, it is also profoundly racialized. Race, Sarah Ahmed shows, is partly a question of what is within reach and ready-to-hand. The reachability of objects—which also includes the availability of some actions, gestures, and so on—racializes the subjects' orientation and the space around them.[50] Ultimately, spaces acquire the *shape* of the bodies that inhabit them as well as their *skin,* in the sense that spaces assume the racial characteristics, the tone, and the orientation of the bodies that are "at-home" within them. This is why we can talk about "white" institutions regardless of the presence of some inner diversity. Whiteness in this sense is "world-making"; it creates a world where only some bodies can feel at home. And some bodies certainly do.

Black things

While whiteness is reified into a property—or an orientation that is world-making and therefore intrinsically exclusionary (in the sense that no other type of body will feel at home in the world that whiteness has made)—blackness is instead susceptible to being reified into concrete and tangible things. Whether they are made of ceramic, cast iron, or wood, the very materiality of the "blackface" objects—the *collectibles* that feature prominently in *Bamboozled*—is the most suitable way in which to convey the idea of blackness as a "hardened form of subjectivity."[51] This sense of "hardness" applies to the black body as well: ideas about the thickness of black skin, its suitability for labor, and its ability to withstand pain convey commonsensical notions of the thingness of blackness by way of an emphasis on its attachment to material things. In other words, blackness seems capable of making everything harder, less sensitive, and more thing-like, including the subject, as Charles Johnson conveys when he describes his sense of being "slumberous, torpid matter."

In African American art practice and criticism of the last twenty years, there has been an identifiable turn to the material culture of slavery—not only thematically, as in the case of Kara Walker's silhouettes, which I will discuss again later, nor only aesthetically, as in Michael Ray Charles' paintings reproducing the aesthetics of blackface collectibles, but also in installation practices that either recycle original objects or reconstruct the environments of objecthood of which the slaves would have been part. In Fred Wilson's *Metalwork*, a display vitrine where the artist places slave shackles alongside a silver tea set of the same era, there is a suggested exchange between matter (iron for the shackles and silver for the tea set) and "captivity." In part, this happens because of their potential "liquidity" as assets, since both metals could be melted down and refashioned as coins. Even though it is not directly visible in the objects, insofar as they are only part of a racial assemblage, it is the fungibility of blackness that authorizes this exchange, that is, the way in which blackness partakes of the exchangeability and replaceability of the commodity. Whiteness is inalienable by definition, since it is the reification of privilege. Blackness, instead, is endlessly alienable and thus essentially *fungible*.[52]

In her groundbreaking essay "Mama's Baby, Papa Maybe: An American Grammar Book," Hortense Spillers shows how one of the consequences of slavery and the Middle Passage is the production of blackness as a type of living matter, in the sense that the slave is stripped of her body and turned into what she calls "flesh," a fact that marks her availability as raw material. The flesh is the physiological level before one even acquires a "body," which is only possible within a framework of possessive individualism, that is, *as* property. The property-less subject, who is someone else's property, cannot have a body.

She has *flesh*. The flesh too is produced through assemblages, with a series of tools for domination (whips, chains, shackles, and so on) that generate what she calls the "hieroglyphics of the flesh." The slave does not have authorized kin, and gender ultimately matters only as a vehicle to transmit property status from the mother to her children. Thus, the slave is not fully individuated and not fully gendered, since nothing in his/her life can even come close to the patriarchal structure surrounding him/her; further, the African American male is removed from view as a partner and as a father. The *flesh*, then, describes the un-gendered and unsexed existence of the slave.[53]

The concepts of the "object" and the "thing" have recently undergone a scholarly renaissance and are usually evoked in order to ground a non-anthropocentric ontological order in which the human and nonhuman, subjects and objects, are on the same level.[54] Yet, what does it mean for the concepts of "thing" and "object" to be revived in such a way? How do they compare to the conceptualization of the "thing" in slavery? How do they compare to the slave *as* thing and blackness *as* thingness?

Martin Heidegger has theorized that the essence of the "thing" always withdraws from human knowledge because things usually appear to us as tools, which we use rather unthinkingly. As tools, we don't know them and don't care to know them. Tools are present to our attention (in fact, they demand it) only when they malfunction or break. The rest of the time, they are "ready-to-hand," unremarkably present.[55]

In *12 Years a Slave* (Steve McQueen, 2013), when Solomon Northup scans the list of items he has been asked to fetch at the store, he "malfunctions" as a tool; the slave is not supposed to be literate, and, in fact, Solomon has been hiding the fact of his literacy until this very moment, when he cannot resist the urge to read. When slaves speak back—or the commodity "shrieks," as Fred Moten puts it, in part to emphasize that this utterance will not register as articulate speech—they are "broken" tools and become "*present*-at-hand." Their malfunctioning has made them unavoidably present and demanding of attention, but only temporarily, because their blackness ultimately confirms their ontological fungibility; it maintains their "ready-at-handedness" against any evidence to the contrary. While "blackness" might be a "thing" in Heidegger's sense of having an essence that always withdraws from human knowledge, in the context of slavery things are fundamentally *black* in their very "at-handedness," indeed, their fungibility. Blackness remains a sign of subjection as well as "property enjoyment" because it indicates something that is always *at-hand* for use and abuse. As Saidiya Hartman explains, "There is no relation to blackness outside of the terms of its use."[56]

There is a primal scene that has been haunting this question of thingness; it is the beating of Aunt Hester described in Frederick Douglass's autobiography, the 1845 *Narrative of the Life of Frederick Douglass*. This is the primal scene of subjection, usually engaged as evidence that the black subject is born from violence. As he describes the brutal and senseless beating of his Aunt Hester, Douglass recognizes that witnessing this scene was, for him, like passing through a "blood-stained gate" that delivered him to subjecthood; it is the equivalent to the statement "I was born." Importantly, Douglass's moment of birth of himself as a subject requires his own objectification alongside his act of witnessing his aunt's objectification. As a subject, he is made and unmade at the same time.

This scene lies at the beginning of Saidiya Hartman's project in *Scenes of Subjection*, which endeavors first to understand the role of violence in the making of the slave subject and then to show how the same violence continues in a different form after Emancipation. Refraining from reproducing or indulging the spectacular nature of this and similar scenes, Hartman instead opts to focus on apparently benign situations such as moments of slave performances (dancing in the quarters or acting on the minstrel stage, for instance) and the ways slave law constructs the humanity of the slave and the idea of the self-possessed individual through the coupling of formal equality and subjugation. Thus, she shows that subjection can occur in a variety of ways, including "coerced agency" or "simulated contentment." Perversely, it also occurs through the mechanics of empathy, when the abolitionist, for example, empathizes with the slave only to the extent that she can imagine herself in the slave's shoes, thus effectively erasing the latter's grief. In other words, even empathy is a form of "assimilation" in the sense of melancholic incorporation described earlier, and subjection occurs precisely because the suffering subject is always erased. She is fungible because she can be both replaced and exchanged at any moment.

If the slave's fungibility partakes of the ontology of the commodity, this does not mean that this ontology contains her entirely. For Fred Moten, the history of blackness is testament to the fact that objects resist. As Aunt Hester's cries show, the commodity shrieks. The black subject might become so through subjugation and objectification, but she will produce sounds that *cut* this scene differently. After this scene, Douglass shares his admiration for the "rude and incoherent" songs the slaves would sing and holler as they marched to the Great House Farm for the monthly allowance. At the time, he says, he didn't recognize that every tone was a protest, prayer, and complaint. It is the materiality of sound, a sound that does not reach the threshold of what would be recognized as word, that enacts the resistance of the object. In this way, blackness marks both the performance of the object and the performance of humanity.

Ontology, hauntology, and the afterlife of slavery

The concept of reification weighs differently on blackness and whiteness. Blackness, in fact, is bound to capital infinitely more tightly than whiteness and, thus, is also confined to capital's temporality. Particularly, it is the body of the slave that measures and fulfills the time and space of capital. The development of the transatlantic slave trade coincides with the rise of finance capital.[57] The prolonged duration and change in scale of economic transactions occurring across the Atlantic made a number of other adjustments necessary, in turn producing increasingly "speculative" entities as objects of trade. For example, bills of credit and insurance contracts were issued in order to stabilize cash flows and protect investments in the slave trade. The slave was central to the establishment of new forms of "money" and to the way blackness became part of a new political economy of the sign of value—not only as a signifier of difference but also a means of exchange. In some cases, the living, breathing biological body of the slave would perform as currency (as on the West African coast, where goods could be exchanged for slaves) and, in other cases, it was the slave's "virtual" body imagined by an insurance contract that signified "money." Consequently, the body of the slave is tied to different conceptions of time: it can represent a unit of currency or a commodity in the present, but it can also offer an investment and, therefore, a financial return in the future. It can also give rise to entirely speculative value, which is secured in advance by the insurance contract that creates that very value.

Put differently, from the point of view of finance capital, the slave is always already virtually dead—or as good as dead—because her value is secured in advance. Thus, another way to describe the virtual body of the slave is as "spectral," since the ghost of the slave will forever haunt the financial transactions it has made possible and vice versa. The term "specter" more accurately expresses the slave's participation in this complex "hauntological" temporality that extends simultaneously into the past and the future. "Hauntology" is a concept introduced by Jacques Derrida in *Specters of Marx* as a way to describe how, for Marx, ideology and conceptual abstractions haunt the material world (for instance, the way in which the fetish character of the commodity produces the commodity's ghostly animism).[58] The specter is always a *re-apparition*. The circular and recursive aspects of this process, plus the concept of time as something that does not pass but accumulates, are most relevant to Critical Race Theory. Hauntology offers a way to think about the *afterlife* of slavery and how it haunts our present. For instance, in the Supreme Court decision *Citizens United v. Federal Election Commission* (2010), political spending (i.e., money) was conceptualized as the corporation's speech and protected under the First Amendment, and thus the sublime body of the slave, who was not allowed to "speak," reappeared in spectral form. Hauntology has been relevant for black and diasporic art practice as well, both because it offers a model to think about one's relationship to an irretrievable past and as a way to think about how past and present might coexist in the same space or object—as happens in the minstrel mask deployed in *Bamboozled.*[59]

The slave is also spectral in another way. The first representation of the slave occurs through the lens of capital. In the archives of slavery, the body is written and rewritten in a variety of forms but never "represented" in a traditional sense. Rather, slaves were usually recorded simply by gender, age, and quantity (in terms of what they were traded for) or in terms of their prospective value, etc. In this way, the archive of slavery records the numerical violence that gives birth to New World blackness and simultaneously evacuates life from blackness itself.

This logic also informs the visual culture of the Middle Passage. One of its most powerful icons is the *Description* of the slave ship *Brookes* prepared by the London Committee for the Abolition of the Slave Trade (1789) by combining the actual measurements of the slave ship with the customary utilization of its cargo space in a typical transatlantic voyage. This drawing is not a representation of how the slaves would actually be arranged in the ship's hold; rather, it is the visualization of the logic of finance capital according to the conventions of naval architecture. The image, in fact, features schematically drawn bodies as placeholders for a projected profit. Yet, despite the fact that the aesthetic formality of this picture performs the same work of abstraction that finance capital implements upon the living, breathing humans subjected to its logic, the

Description garnered widespread support for the abolitionist cause because it was read naturalistically, as an actual depiction of an actual ship.[60]

There is a profound emptiness at the heart of the archive of slavery because the slave body is recorded only to the extent that it lies at the center of a perverse system of equivalences, embodied in a vast array of texts and social practices—the slave ledger, the ship's logbook, the insurance contract, the bills of exchange—all of which are artifacts that record and express finance capital's ruthless logic of abstraction. Thus, there is nothing in these documents that can bring the traded men, women, and children to visibility. Only their movements can be beheld: their coerced transportation, the transactions they made possible, and their conversion into money.

Hartman has addressed this question of absence by seeking to reconstruct the death of two slave girls we know about only because the captain was put on trial to determine the circumstances of their deaths. This fact shows how the archive of slavery reverses the logic of representation insofar as what is not *there* in the archive has the chance to be *living*. Consequently, the archive itself has to be approached against its own logic. How might these two girls' presence return to an archive that refuses to record their lives? How might they be liberated from the representational violence through which we came to know of their existence (through their death)? One strategy is to read what Hartman calls the "asterisked archive of the middle passage" while looking for discrepancies and traces of what has not been recorded—for example, an asterisk next to a ledger listing indicating that one female slave "*says she was born free* at Newtown, Long Island."[61]

The question of representation

This sense of a violent and suffocating archive has influenced how black feminist scholarship has understood the problem of visual representation. Here, too, there is a primal scene: the visual exploitation and abuse of the black female body occurs with the exhibition of Saartjie Baartman—the "Hottentot Venus"—a Quena woman who was paraded and displayed in Europe in the first half of the nineteenth century. Baartman was an object of perverse curiosity that allowed audiences to seemingly access and assess, but in reality actively *construct*, the "primitive" other. The visual fascination surrounding her body shows the power of the imbrication of ethnographic, spectacular, and pornographic gazes. It also compounds a metonymic process that Fanon explained is already at work when the black body is encountered in the field of vision as the mechanism whereby an *individual* black body stands in for *every* black body. More specifically, the fixation on *one* part of that body—the penis in black males and the buttocks in black females—makes that specific part stand in metonymically for the whole.

Baartman constitutes a recurring primal scene for the articulation of how the "problem of the visual" weighs differently on the black *female* body, which is *wounded* in specific ways by continued misrepresentations. In the black feminist archive, the visual is not only a site of trauma and injury but also a "negative scene of instruction," a type of pedagogy, because of how it actively *teaches* how to mistreat black women.[62] Two main issues meet in this assessment: one is the question of the politics of representation, and the other is the idea of the agency of the visual, that is, the extent to which representation is a form of action.

The question of representation is the most vexing for minority groups because, at its most basic level, representation implies both a form of "speaking for" and a form of depiction. It is both political and aesthetic at the same time. For minority groups that have limited access to either, the two terms are most often conflated.[63] Minority artists are burdened with the obligation to act as proxy for a larger group, and the reception of their work is overdetermined by a number of external considerations that have little to do with its form or value as art. Kobena Mercer has described this accumulation of demands as the *burden of representation*, a situation that expresses the pernicious encroachment of identity politics into the aesthetic assessment of minority art. Black art, film, and cultural expressions are rarely met and discussed on formal grounds; instead, they are subjected to the extratextual expectations that a black artist should only explore "black themes," that she would pour her identity into her work, and, ultimately, that she would produce *recognizably* "black" art. But what might "black" ultimately mean in this context?

Consider the idea of "Black Film Studies." The term "black" applies pressure to both "film" and "film studies" through a tension between describing the object, that is, studies of "black film," and the positionality of the scholarship, that is, "black studies" of film. In each case, the location of the term *black* reveals how it is fraught with deep tensions. On one hand, it poses as a representation—in the sense of offering a "portrayal" of that to which it refers—and on the other, it is epithetical: something becomes "black" in the moment it is named so. On one hand, it appears to want to consolidate some essential notion of blackness or black people (or a black way of doing scholarship, or a definitively clear concept of what makes a black film, and so on). On the other hand, it appears highly flexible and fluctuating and, therefore, seemingly in need of some form of essentialization.

The tension between these poles is at the root of Stuart Hall's influential essay, "What is this 'black' in black popular culture?," which attempted to balance the expansiveness of the signifier "black" in popular culture—which comprises a variety of diverse, contradictory, and always shifting forms—with, on the other hand, the demand for the signifier "black" to articulate the cultural identities of ethnic outsiders in British society. In this essay, Hall champions its instability and insists that it is the concept of the "popular" that fixes the authenticity of mass cultural forms, giving the impression that it could lead to the recovery of "something pure" one "could live by," or that "black" could function as a test of authenticity.

Popular culture, cautions Hall, is a mythologized space, a theater of desires, and a place to play with multiple identifications. In fact, the fluidity of popular culture shows us that there is no identity or life that is lived outside of representation. Negotiating a place within existing discourses forms identities; identities are not found before and outside those discourses. They are "unstable points of identification or suture" and, thus, identities are ultimately mobile, not fixed; they are a form of *positioning*, not an essence; a form of *becoming*, not a type of being; they are *produced*, not discovered; *narrated*, not simply found.

In film and media studies, this conflation of the political and aesthetic valences of representation has emerged in the form of a reliance on realist aesthetics to communicate the true black experience. This means that, alongside being representative, the artist is also expected to be representational—not abstract, opaque, or oblique, but easily legible and straightforwardly mimetic. An experimental filmmaker, for example, is often less recognizably black than a classically narrative one. The artist's identity, furthermore, is imagined to appear transparently and effortlessly in her work. Or, seen from the opposite side, the work is expected to be mimetically reflective of an artist's identity.

The burden of mimesis

The idea of mimesis is a complicated site of conflict. In Western art, "mimesis" is the cornerstone of a realist aesthetics and is attached to the idea that the work has to be a reenactment (or imitation) of the "real" world, thus reconciling the political and aesthetic valences of representation. The more mimetic the work is, the more political it is as well. Yet, complete mimesis is unattainable. Specifically for the racial subject, mimesis is an injunction, not a choice, to imitate dominant modes of behaving in the world so that one's difference will become unremarkable. And yet, the very ambivalence of dominant discourse demands that difference be maintained. In other words, the other has to be familiar enough to not be entirely frightening, incomprehensible, or unrecognizable, and yet different enough to be clearly marked as other. As Homi Bhabha described it in the context of the colonial situation, this is the injunction to "be like" and "not be like," to be the same but not quite, the same but not white. Unavoidably, then, the image that the "native" returns to the settler will be a form of *mimicry*—a mixture of sameness and difference—it will imitate and "repeat" with a difference that, constitutively, can never be eliminated. The colonized, in other words, is forced to occupy an impossible space of ambivalence that grants them neither identity nor difference; they must mimic an image that they cannot fully assume.[64]

The deeper paradox is here: the other is never encountered directly, outside of representation and discourse—Fanon has shown how wrapped up in fantasies and fears this encounter is—and yet she is always expected to be "the thing" itself *before* any discourse or representation. The representations that she produces, in turn, are supposed to perfectly mimic not the discourse she is wrapped into but rather what she is expected to be, that is, the thing itself. The other and her cultural expressions are constantly oscillating between the inside and outside of representation and constantly expected to be what is untouched by it.

Stereotypes and representation

Stereotype is one of the most charged terms in critical race discourse; it is, quite straightforwardly, the stigma of the disenfranchised. To be stereotyped means to not only be overdetermined (I am slave of my own appearance, says Fanon) but also *signify* the very process of overdetermination. To be stereotyped entails being that which is always already known and can be endlessly narrated. On a commonsensical level, stereotypes are understood as powerful types of misrepresentations. Usually, they are negative, but there can also be positive stereotypes. As Fanon's discussion of mental colonization makes clear, stereotypes are also images that one has interiorized: they can be the other inside the self. From an etymological standpoint, however, stereotyping refers to a typographic technique whereby pages constituted of mobile type would be converted into a unique slate of cast iron. Thus, etymologically, stereotypes fixed molds used for reproduction and therefore embody the tension between fixity and duplication that characterizes them most strongly.

In a film or media studies class focused on race, the first thing that students want to discuss or write about is the "representation of . . . [fill in the blank]" in some media or genre. For them, media representations always raise the question of "is it me?" or "not me?" Fanon says, "I cannot go to a film without seeing myself. I wait for me. In the interval, just before the film starts, I wait for me."[65] Here, it is ultimately the "me" that carries the weight of the conflict and negotiation he has to somehow resolve. This passage has been used to ground a theory of media and art spectatorship because, if anything, the Black is always also the spectator of a scene within which she is constructed as image. In the Antilles, Fanon writes, the native will go to a *Tarzan* film and identify with Tarzan; seeing the same film in France, she will fear the appearance of the natives and recognize herself on screen through them as a stain instead. The screen will no longer function as a mirror to be enjoyed, but as an opaque surface instead.

The temporality of this process is crucial: because of the colonial construction of the *imago* of the Black, the black subject is locked into a past that overdetermines her present. She is the prisoner of an accumulation of socially constructed images associated with her blackness. Importantly, Fanon describes himself as one who "waits," thus expressing his experience of suspension before an *imago* that is always already there and revealing the anticipation of something that is already foreclosed. Within this "hellish cycle," the present is always the reappearance of the past. The Black is both permanently belated and always already there. As Kara

Keeling puts it, the Black described by Fanon exists "in the interval," a temporal suspension that matches the suspension experienced once he encounters the imago that the other has projected onto him: "Look, a Negro!"[66]

When students want to discuss "representation," they are working through these questions. They do it by exercising their ability to identify stereotypes. However, stereotypes gain power from their constant repetition so that, at times, even the critical act of identifying them might end up becoming complicit with their proliferation. In other words, just like the molds they originally indicated, stereotypes reproduce by virtue of the constant repetition of their own fixity. Thus, the endless recurrence of the eureka moment in stereotype analysis—"Look, Aunt Jemima!"; "Look, an Uncle Tom!"; "Look, a Jezebel!"—might not be so different from the endless repetition of the moment of visual fixation identified by Fanon: "Look, a Negro."

Here is a practical exercise that will highlight this fact: ban the use of the term stereotype in your class. Students are still allowed to discuss stereotypes, but they cannot call them so. This rhetorical constraint eventually produces a descriptive effort that shifts attention from what the stereotype supposedly *represents* to what it *is* and what it *does*, how it *works*, and what it *achieves*.

Here is the opposite exercise. I have my students read Toni Morrison's short story "Recitatif," which she discusses in her book, *Playing in the Dark*, as "an experiment in the removal of all racial codes from a narrative about two characters of different races for whom racial identity is crucial."[67] This is a brilliantly misleading statement. In fact, Morrison did not remove all racial codes but left them unattributed, giving the reader the task of determining to whom they belong and, even more provocatively, which codes are racial and which aren't. "Recitatif" follows two characters, Roberta and Twyla, from childhood to adulthood. It is narrated by Twyla, and it begins with her arrival at the New York orphanage St. Bonaventure, where she immediately "feels sick to her stomach" upon discovering that she has been put in a room with a girl of a "whole different race." The story, however, never tells us what this "other race" is, but, because it expresses the characters' reactions to each other, it justifiably employs a racially charged language. Statements such as "My mother said [. . .] that they never washed their hair and they smelled funny," or "Everything is so easy for them. They think they own the world," read as racially motivated. But are they?

Despite their difference, Roberta and Twyla hit it off because they have some important things in common; for example, they are not actual orphans. Their mothers are alive, although unable to care for them: Roberta's is "sick" and Twyla's "dances all night." After this initial bonding experience over their mothers' absence, Roberta and Twyla meet again several times over the span of thirty years. At each encounter, the reader is also given a new set of contradictory "descriptors." For example, in the 1960s Roberta has "huge hair," and she is on her way to a Jimi Hendrix concert. Twyla, instead, waits tables at a Howard Johnson's. Each encounter reveals how racial strife has created a wedge between them that overrides the initial bond they had established.

Here is where the exercise is most useful. Invariably, readers of this short story will attempt to "discover" the character's racial identity from some supposed clue in the text. This means that they will have to leverage some of these descriptors as identifiers of race. Some of them are fairly innocuous—one of the mothers brings spam to her visit at the orphanage, a sign of her whiteness, by most accounts—but others are not: Whose hair goes unwashed? Who smells funny?

I write my students' comments on a white board; the two names, Twyla and Roberta, go on top, and then a column for whiteness and one for blackness underneath, so that we can keep track of what clues are being given in one direction or another. As the conversation ensues in class, two things happen: different students want to count different things as black or white and the descriptors end up moving from one racial column to the other quite easily. One begins to realize that, as Stuart Hall argued, race itself is a "floating signifier;" it is more like a language than a thing that exists biologically in the natural world. More profoundly, however, nobody can even begin to identify these descriptors without mobilizing deep-seated stereotypes. Again, who smells funny? Yet, during this process, the students also realize how they are actively *building* the racial identity of the two characters by *fleshing out*—in the sense of attaching a body to—a series of descriptors that could, at least theoretically, remain floating. They are also modulating their own sensorium in this quest. What emerges, then, is not so much the content of the stereotype, which the students become painfully weary of evoking, but the cultural work it performs: the stereotype appears functional to our desire to continue to think of race as a form of *representation* of difference.

One of the strongest criticisms levied against *Bamboozled* is that it unleashes pernicious stereotypes it cannot ultimately contain. The idea that stereotypes can be unleashed, like wild animals or a virus, speaks to their vitality. W. J. T. Mitchell, who has theorized the loves and lives of images, approaches the stereotype as the prototype of the desiring image. Stereotypes are representations that appear instead to be living things themselves. And, the more "true-to-life" they appear, the more they multiply, just like living things. At the same time, stereotypes are capacious receptacles for desire. Without our desire, the stereotype is sterile; infused with our desire, it is vibrant, believable, and seductive—it comes "alive." The stereotype wants precisely what it lacks—life, animation, vitality.[68] Yet, this is also what it gets every time it is evoked. Stereotypes are therefore intensely desiring images with a number of "wants": they want to circulate unboundedly, they want to trump all other images, and they want to be taken for real.

When we think of the stereotype as a stilted representation, no mobility, disarticulation, or negotiation appears possible. Regarding the invocation of a black experience that lies untouched before representation, Stuart Hall explained that "there *is* a politics there to be struggled for. But the invocation of a guaranteed black experience behind it will not produce that politics."[69]

Stereotypes, ambivalence, and desire

The stereotype's fixity is a symptom of its profound ambivalence—the awareness of its constructedness and its inadequacy in managing the affects and desires that it reifies. The stereotype partakes of the same logic of the fetish and, like the fetish, is related to the discovery of a difference that traumatically disrupts the fantasy of an original sameness. Stereotypes express specific desires toward difference: to make it *present, visible, knowable*, and to *fixate* it. Ultimately, the stereotype is not a representation but a scene of subject formation; it is not simply the object of desire but its setting; not just the reflection of a false image but the projection of a need for closure, presence, fullness, and, ultimately, a stability that the stereotype itself can never fully deliver.[70]

Once we recognize the ambivalence of the stereotype, we can also recognize our own ambivalence toward it. This is something Kobena Mercer describes in his writing on Robert Mapplethorpe's photographs of black male nudes, which he first encountered when a friend gave him a copy of *Black Males*. Mercer initially read Mapplethorpe's work through the idea of the stereotype as fetish and, thus, criticized the photographer's objectification of the black body. In *The Man in a Polyester Suit* (1980)—which is a cropped photograph of a black man's midsection adorned in a polyester suit with a large penis hanging from his open fly—Mercer discovered the same dynamic of disavowal of fetishism: "I *know* it's not true that all black men have big penises, *but still*, in my photographs they do."[71] Mercer's initial position held that the pleasure of these photographs was to be found in their openness about how they fetishize racial difference and how this fetishism would "lubricate" the reproduction of racial otherness as a form of mastery of the other.

In his later writing, however, Mercer recognized his own desire for the same object of the gaze and his own longing to be inscribed in the sexual fantasy staged by Mapplethorpe's images. His earlier reading did not fully account for the profound ambivalence of the work and attributed it entirely to the author. Instead, by focusing on the author's implication in the work—at least in terms of laying bare his own desire, as well as the specific reversibility of the gaze and shifting positions of identification available in homoerotic visual representations—he discovered that Mapplethorpe's images offered ways to investigate profound cultural and social ambivalences, including those implicit in the generic constraints and codes of high art and portrait photography. Mapplethorpe produced hybrid images—here mixing nature (the penis) with culture (the suit) but also fear (of its size) with the desire for crossing the boundaries that separate high culture from low culture and that separate the proper subject of the "nude" from the "crude"—that offered a subversive strategy that disrupted the traditional binaries within which race and gender are encoded. The photographer's implication of himself in these images ultimately pointed to an even more profound ambivalence between the desire for the other as a form of incorporation and the way in which signifiers of a degraded racial otherness are assimilated into the construction of one's cultural identity. "What is it about whiteness," asked Mercer, "that makes the white subject want to be black?"[72]

Desire for the stereotype

From the mid-1990s onward, a number of artists have been engaged in what has been called the "new art of the stereotype." The most controversial among them is silhouette artist Kara

Walker, who, at the age of 28 in 1997, won a MacArthur genius award for her life-size installations of scenes of plantation life. Executed with tremendous skill and attention to detail, her silhouettes depict scenarios of unmistakable depravity as a way to uncover the complicated mental landscape of the master–slave relation in the American South. From an ontological point of view, her figures are highly unstable because they do not clearly indicate where they are coming from: fantasy, nightmare, recollection, repetition, projection, or remembrance. Furthermore, even though they are silhouettes, they look like shadows cast by actual bodies onto the gallery wall, thus making unclear the involvement of the body in their production and destination: Was a body there, or is it being conjured up by the naturalism of the silhouettes themselves? They are also deliberately hauntological insofar as they imply a complicated chronology in the history of the visual arts by using an archaic pre-cinematic and pre-photographic form to create highly cinematic effects in a post-cinematic moment; as such, they are images that always act as re-apparitions. Walker's immediate success with white critics and art collectors triggered a vitriolic critical response from African American artist Betye Saar and other artists of her generation, who sought support for a boycott of Walker's work.[73] Saar's complaint was directed at the irresponsibility of reanimating stereotypes that are best left dormant and the immorality of unleashing imagery that takes on a life of its own.

Michael Ray Charles, who worked as a visual consultant for *Bamboozled*, has been subjected to a similar, although less intense, critique.[74] His art began in response to a black figurine a friend gave him, a blackface collectible just like those that populate the film's mise-en-scène. He was so intrigued by the object that he began making art that investigates the object's aesthetic parameters and the social fantasies it attempts to project; in particular, he explores the way blackface art provides an image of race relations modeled after the property relations of slavery. A great part of the cultural work performed by his paintings resides in their mimicry of commodity objects and the visual culture of turn-of-the-century advertising. His paintings reproduce—but with a strategic difference, namely, a blackface aesthetic—the aesthetics of early advertisements, circus posters, magazine covers (in particular, Norman Rockwell's 1940s ads for *Saturday Evening Post*), children's puzzles, and other objects, thus emphasizing both how blackness invites a slippage from image to thing and how blackness is constructed in assemblage with objects, by dancing with things. In mimicking their models this way, Charles' paintings perform an act of historical excavation that reveals how American visual and material culture employs blackness to deliver tangible forms for commodity status. Charles insists that these images are white as much as black, and his paintings strive to sustain the ambiguous sources of their fantastical scenarios. Like Walker's silhouettes, it is not clear whose fantasy one is observing.

David Levinthal's photographs of "Sambo art," some of which appear in *Bamboozled*, have sometimes been discussed in the same vein. In his introduction to Levinthal's book, *Blackface*, Manthia Diawara argues that this type of engagement with stereotypes makes yet another understanding of the role of desire available—the desire *for* the stereotype. Levinthal's art photography, in particular, lets the object determine the terms of its encounter and, therefore, unfolds the *fetish* into a *scene* of desire. Several characteristics of Levinthal's photography achieve this effect. First, the decision to place these figurines against a deeply black background and to shoot them from a slightly low angle accentuates their monumentality as well as the materiality of their blackness, especially when the light shines on their polished surfaces. Zooming into parts of the figurine's body that are already deformed or exaggerated further highlights how stereotypes work with "pastiche, caricature, and symbols." The location of these figures within an engulfing blackness makes viewers aware of how they must contribute to the process of making out the contours of the figurines' faces. As they do so, the spectators realize the complicity of their desire, and they become aware that the stereotype has been located in a dramatic situation; the figurine then appears "active" and able to engage with its surroundings. Ultimately, Levinthal *sets the toys in motion* "with a cinematic effect" and thus awakens the histories congealed in these objects.[75]

One cannot resist the stereotype without creating another one. Cultural theorists and artists who condemn the work of Kara Walker or Michael Ray Charles have assigned themselves "the burden of representation," taking on the role of cultural police to make sure that black art has only positive content and avoids, or actively deconstructs, stereotypes. What would it mean, instead, to recognize the work of desire that animates the stereotype and to further animate such work? What does it mean to desire the scene of desire? Desiring the scene of desire means to be willing to deal with the formal complexity of stereotypes, their intrinsic ambivalence, and the multiple trajectories of identification and desire they afford.

Look, Aunt Delilah! Stereotype and commodity form

To understand the connection between the stereotype and the commodity, we need to regard them through a simultaneously material and semiotic lens, that is, through the lens of the political economy of the sign.[76] From this standpoint, stereotypes participate in the logic of the commodity form where "form," in this case, highlights the commodity's ability to exchange. The stereotype's ambivalence is also the source of its *currency*, insofar as stereotypes participate in a symbolic economy as both agents and channels (means and media) of circulation.

The stereotype enters this economy of exchange by way of *likeness*. It exchanges because it traffics in some degree of sameness or similarity, or both, either at the level of content— the stereotype always triggers the same ideas, connotations, and associations, for example, the thug, the mammie figure, etc.—or entirely on the surface at the level of the visual signifier, such as when, in *Imitation of Life*, we see Delilah's transformation into the pancake trademark logo and, eventually, the large Times Square neon sign. *Likeness* is not a feature of the object but rather a historically situated product of visual culture, which can train us to see things as *alike*. The "likeness" of the stereotype gives it the ability to move across different sensorial regimes and eventually exchange for (or "harden" into) a real thing. For example, burnt cork makeup is the reified version of skin blackness turned into a thing, and, even more intensely, it becomes a blackface coating in stereotypical artifacts. What is difficult to comprehend nowadays is the extent to which these objects were conceived for everyday use, demanding some kind of intimacy with their user and encouraging repeated interaction, even simply by requiring regular touching, which ultimately becomes a version of what bell hooks has described as "eating the other." Moreover, contemporary observers may miss that the objects' intended "humor" depends on deploying blackness as a legitimate outlet for aggression.

Blackface

As a concept, theatrical genre, practice, and aesthetic construct, blackface puts strain on the concept of representation and particularly troubles the idea of the stereotype *as* representation. Even though minstrelsy is undoubtedly one of the most demeaning cultural forms in US history, its complex dynamics cannot be explained simply as a case of stereotypicality. Yet, just like the stereotype, it is by passing itself off as a type of representation that blackface has performed much of its complex and troubling cultural work.

The minstrel show began in the late 1820s in the context of the northern urban working class and it was the first form of mass (visual and sonic) culture about slavery. In it, white performers (at first) and black performers (later) would wear blackface makeup made from burnt cork to cover visible skin and would perform a series of songs, dances, and sketches framed as providing an unobstructed view of blacks in their supposed natural environments—that is, conditions of servitude and Southern plantation life. Thus, even though it passes itself off as a mimetic cultural form, blackface minstrelsy is a highly reflexive practice of mimicry and, therefore, it is also a reflection on questions of representation as such.

Leveraging the expected mimetic relation between skin color and racial identity, blackface minstrelsy turns the epidermal signifier into a man-made mask. This mask in turn authorizes a performance of blackness. The possibility of *doing* blackness highlights the idea of appropriation, which is only available if blackness is at least somewhat performative already.

Blackface is an aesthetic form that deploys a chromatic blackness to signify race, albeit not directly. From the point of view of signification, blackface is a second-degree racial signifier because its first reference is not "race" but the epidermality of race. If black skin operates as the index of race, then burnt-cork makeup signifies it iconically, so that blackface becomes an image *of* blackness *as* image of race. From an aesthetic point of view, blackface also offers a specific hermeneutics of the surface that duplicates and fetishizes the social function of skin color. It is a hermeneutics of face value, in the sense that value, meaning, identity, etc., are expected to be found on, and therefore read off of, the body's surface. Blackface is a way for the body to wear an image of its own superficialization and to invite an interpretive reading of that surface.

There is a primal scene that articulates the origin of blackface. It involves an entertainer who went by the name of T. D. Rice. One of the most influential accounts of this moment comes from Eric Lott, who describes the dynamic of fear and desire, fascination and exploitation that sustains minstrelsy as a kind of "love and theft."[77]

One day, circa 1828, T. D. Rice convinced a black man named Cuff to accompany him to the theater. Once there, Rice blackened up his face with burnt cork, ordered Cuff to disrobe, and put on Cuff's clothing. The white man took the black man's clothes and wore makeup that would signify the other's skin, insofar as it is the most evident outward sign of his otherness (love). But in performing this act of fascination, Rice was also stealing from Cuff: he was fascinated with the commodified black body and understood blackness within a logic of fungibility, as something that was detachable from Cuff and available for his taking (theft). The black body itself is considered a commodity object, and its blackness is commodified one more time. Indeed, for Lott, the commodity form is minstrelsy's *blackest* thing in the sense that not only is blackness a commodity, but also *commodification is black*. Furthermore, the blackening of the face links the performer to commodity objects and metaphorically turns the top of the body into its bottom, hardening consciousness or thought into animal-like physicality.

As it unravels on stage, the minstrel show also becomes a potentially homoerotic affair between male bodies, since male entertainers had to impersonate female characters who were often depicted as having a devouring and insatiable sexual appetite. These impersonations tamed an obvious interest and attraction toward black women and, in the process, created a collective, homoerotic, masturbation fantasy. In other words, transgressions across racial and gender lines highlight an important effect of minstrelsy: the idea that blackface would become a vehicle to enter a different (and immoral, or at least amoral) universe where the most grotesque and vulgar acts could be performed and the most forbidden desires could be acted out. Simply put, blackface initiated, licensed, and channeled a "walk on the wild side." The melancholic elements of this relation are vividly exemplified in the final scene of David Cronenberg's *M. Butterfly* (1993), when Gallimard's performance and suicide take place as an embodiment of his lover, whose body he never really knew.

Wearing the minstrel mask is cause for profound anxiety. The black performer fears that the mask will adhere so tightly to his face that he will be unable to take it off. The white performer, instead, fears he will be swallowed up by the abyss that opens on the other side of the mask; he worries that, as Ralph Ellison described it, "he is not simply *miming* a personification of his disorder and chaos, but *that he will become in fact that which he intends only to symbolize.*"[78] With this idea of the *contagious nature of mimicry*, Ellison points to a specific affect that seems associated with the "adherence" of blackness— an idea of contamination, stickiness, and engulfment that is heavily and strategically deployed in *Bamboozled*.

Seen from the outside, blackface is clearly a mask, but, if we focus on its function, it appears more like a channel for interracial contact. As a mask, blackface is an instrument of exteriority, a reflecting mirror where a complex web of social, material, and discursive relations become visible. As a channel, however, blackface appears more like an interiority, a potentially bottomless hole the performer enters upon donning the minstrel mask. Blackface is also pervaded by a tension between hypervisibility (for its spectacular nature) and under-visibility (insofar as it renders the performer's face invisible).

Blackface as mass culture

Michael Rogin has argued that transformative moments in the history of American cinema (from popular, critical, narrative, industrial, aesthetic, and formal points of view) have all organized themselves around forms of "appropriative identification" with blackness.[79] He regards the minstrel show as the most popular original form of national mass culture. Blackface and black impersonation were particularly instrumental for the assimilation of immigrant groups, especially Jews, who played the role of the outsider in order to project an image of harmonious fluidity of boundaries between black and white, thus fostering their own assimilation into a white identity. Central to this process is the recurrence, particularly in pre-World War II Hollywood musicals, of a scene where the artist puts on blackface makeup. Rogin argues that this moment functions as a *primal scene* in which viewers are shown the secret of blackness as fetish. This scene is not constructed to demystify the fetish but rather to empower it by showing the moment in which it is being put on. It is also a crucial rite of passage, from "immigrant" to "American," which condenses the maintenance of white supremacy through a fantasy of integration.

As a national form of mass culture, minstrelsy should be regarded as providing a popular aesthetics because of the way it constructs "a people" through its spectacular form. The audience comes together in identifying with, or projecting their working class status onto, the portrayal of the black slave in order to articulate their alignment of wage labor with slave labor, all the while reaping the benefits of what DuBois called the "wages of whiteness." Indeed, whiteness and "a people" are the paradoxical end product of the show itself. The audience comes together as "a people" precisely in reaction to the spectacle of amalgamation the minstrel offers by dramatizing the miscegenation of the American social body before its eyes.[80]

Visual fixation and photographic ontology

Blackness is at the center of several processes of reification whereby its flexibility and relationality are hardened or congealed into a fixed form. Whether it is as a stereotype, a fetish, a commodity, or a material substance, reification variously occurs in the practice of blackface. The precondition for these processes is the very fixity of the epidermal signifier for the way it reduces identity to a visual fact. This is the reason Fanon has described the moment of epidermalization and visual fixation through a photographic metaphor: the gaze of the other fixes him, he writes, "the same way *you fix a preparation with a dye.*"[81] As anyone who has developed a photograph knows, the final form of the photograph (its contrast, for example) is the product of the arbitrary interruption of a process of development and is thereby a deliberate act of fixation of the image. In this sense, "photography" not only describes the process of becoming an image but also the abrupt conclusion of this process. This is the fixation to which Fanon wants to call attention. His metaphor also evokes the idea of a chemical reaction—the "alchemy" of race—whereby the epidermis acts as a photosensitive surface that registers and exposes an otherwise invisible racial identity.

This is the Fanonian moment: the point at which blackness is visually fixated, and, just like in the process of developing a photograph, the image's becoming is halted, and the image acquires its permanent form. More broadly, the Fanonian moment is also the moment in which this image is found troubling; it is the point at which the black body is received as a disturbance in the field of vision, a disturbance that is created precisely by the reaction that Fanon describes in the child: "Look, a Negro." The circularity of this process is important: the black body troubles a field of vision that has already constructed it as troubling. This circularity is what Fanon has described as being overdetermined from the outside, that is, being judged by a predetermined reading that *over*runs any other consideration.[82]

The relationship between race and photography is similarly overdetermined by a number of factors that have important repercussions for how the visual "fact of blackness" grounds the supposed self-evidence of race. From the point of view of visual culture, photography is the medium that consolidated the idea of skin color as visual evidence of otherwise invisible differences. As the natural companion of nineteenth-century disciplines—such as ethnography, anthropology, phrenology, criminology, and physiognomy—which were organized around the desire to *see* difference and to establish iconographies and criteria for recognizing difference at a glance, photography had an active role in producing race as a *visualizable fact* and provided a visual technology that sutured race onto the body.

The idea of photography as a transparent medium is also overdetermined; its "transparency" results from photography's tendency to efface itself as a medium and give the illusion of unmediated and objective access to what it represents. As a technology of vision that contributed to constructing the visual evidence of race, photography's purported transparency was immediately put to the service of the panoptic structure of segregation.[83]

The relationship between photography and race is also overdetermined by the expectation that they share the same semiotic structure—that is, that they are both indexes, or *traces*. Within the typology of signs identified by Charles Sanders Peirce—index, icon, and symbol—the index is the sign most often understood as being produced by contact—footprints in the sand, for instance—whether this contact is visible or not (for example, a weather wane moved by the invisible touch of wind is also an indexical sign). In this view, the photographic sign, understood as a specific combination of the indexical and iconic orders, is both metonymical and metaphorical; it is both a trace and a copy of the world. Thinking about a photograph as an index entails focusing on the idea of continuity between the world and the photographic image (rays of light touching a photosensitive surface, for example, or the object touching the viewer *through* its photographic mediation, as Roland Barthes described it in *Camera Lucida*) and therefore considering the truth of the photograph as dependent on this continuity.[84] Within this framework, just as a photograph is considered a *trace* of the real, skin color is similarly seen as primarily a *trace* of racial difference.

Ultimately, photography and race support the other's epistemology, naturalizing it as fundamentally self-evident. Photography corroborates the idea that race leaves its trace on the body's epidermis, whereas the visibility of the black body "fleshes out" the photographic process, reproducing it in bodily form, as if race had made an impression onto an otherwise unmarked skin, just like light makes an impression and forms an image on a photosensitive support. Thus, race and photography also share similar processes of exteriorization, and they both produce legible surfaces.

The emergence of photography as a privileged mode of perception and expression in the mid-nineteenth century coincides with commodity-based market capitalism and the dominant aesthetic mode of realism. The photograph becomes the standard for all "realisms" and is central to a new economy of cultural exchange. As much as photography appears to secure an unfettered and direct connection to the "thing," it also institutes a system of visual exchange between images and things, as well as between images and other images. Jean-Louis Comolli describes this function of photography as the "general equivalent," which is the same way Marx describes money. The photograph, therefore, becomes "the money of the real."[85] The very idea of "money" emphasizes the awareness that photography abstracts that which it depicts, somehow acting as a universal medium of exchange. In this sense, therefore, "photography" expresses many of the same desires and dynamics already involved in our relationship to money—for example, the fact that money makes referential claims but has no referential value and the way in which money is an empty system of representation that represents itself *as a system* with each monetary transaction.

This fact sheds new light onto the crisis of referentiality, which, for many theorists, is attached to the rise of the digital image, as if digitality had forever severed photography's (indexical) connection to the world. In reality, the possibility for photographs to work as "money," as well as our tendency to take them at face value, has always been part of the very system of visual exchange that photography instituted in the first place. The analog and the digital express two different, but overlapping, imaginations of the relationship between the image and the world: the former predicated on the expectation of a material continuity with the world, and the latter haunted by the idea of the world's reducibility to code. Ultimately, however, the image we face is always analogic—if we were to look at digital code, we would not recognize it as an image—and it is through this analog interface that we engage with the image's content and truth-value.

Finally, is a digitally photographed black body any less black? Perhaps, then, if there is a specific trait that is attached to the digital, it is the possibility of emphasizing the money-form of photography—photography not as delivering a content we immediately attach to the world but rather as a means of exchange. Ultimately, thinking about photography as the money of the real might help us think about race as the money of the real as well, with blackness as its primary currency and scene of exchange.

Habeas Corpus: Blackness and photographic presence

This approach to photography and race as money of the real is very important for the way *Bamboozled* mobilizes various kinds of screen blackness to initiate scenes of exchange. Yet, there is a photographic effect that exceeds this framework and is the result of the overdetermined relation between photography and race—specifically, the way one has corroborated and "fleshed out" the other by strengthening its truth-effects and its ability to produce an effect of presence. By "effect of presence," I mean the ability for photography (in its broadest sense, considered in a historical continuum that comprises both still and moving images, as well as photochemical, electronic, and digital images) to efface its mediation to the point that the viewer has a sense of sharing the same space as what they see. This is hardly a question that photographic ontology can answer, and it is the product of a contingent relation between the type of technological mediation (the photographic image, the video image, and the digital image) and the degree and type of stillness and movement of the black body in it. It also depends on the ideological and institutional framing of the image, which might absorb, redirect, or, most often, highlight this sense of presence.

Spike Lee's *Clockers* (1995) addresses these issues. It opens with people gathered at the scene of a crime. Standing behind police tape—"POLICE LINE. DO NOT CROSS"—are men, women, and children, looking dismayed, shaking their heads, or simply staring. Shots of this impromptu crowd alternate with extreme close-ups, swirling zooms, and canted angles onto restaged crime scene photographs of dead "clockers" (i.e., drug dealers) as well as graffiti and murals marking the spot of a violent death. *Clockers* has been read as a reflection on the 'hood film—a cycle that begins in 1991 with films such as *Boyz N the Hood*, *New Jack City*, and *Menace II Society*— with which the cycle arguably concludes. The film engages with the possibilities and constraints of the genre while offering a critique of the continued expectations of realism, authenticity, and (especially) grittiness in black cinematic representations. *Clockers* approaches these issues in part through the question of technologically mediated presence. The film begins with a small archive of media representations of black violent deaths framed around the example of something that the mediated image cannot do: put the seer and the seen in the same space. This opening sequence stages competing types of presence: the physical presence of the people gathered at the scene of the crime and the graffiti and murals shot on-location; photographic presence, that is, the camera's examination of restaged crime scene photographs; and filmic presence, that is, the way the film itself archives all these mediated images and scenes or signs of witnessing. The sequence shows that the question of presence has at least two important valences. One is the expectation that representation will be entirely transparent and effectively deliver "the thing." The other is that this "delivery" would produce the sense that seer and seen are in each other's presence, sharing the same physical space. This, in turn, can elicit a variety of responses, from fear to horror, disgust to arousal, or anxiety to excitement.

Each medium is capable of fostering a different sense of presence, and, in this opening sequence, Lee brings together several mediated and unmediated encounters to encourage a reflection on the way each mediatic configuration differently articulates the relationship between the viewing subject, vision, and the visual object. Being in the presence of the slain body, Lee suggests, is different from looking at a crime scene photograph, which affords the critical distance necessary for an investigative gaze. Furthermore, looking at a restaged crime scene photograph as part of a narrative film directly interrogates the burden of representation inherent in any racial image and the way its mediation (technological, generic, or formal) tends to be effaced. Lee takes note of the grittiness expected from the genre and delivers it with the film's first image: the extreme close-up of a gunshot wound—wet and vibrantly red—which, for a moment, fills the entire screen.

Taking the clue from *Clockers*, I will briefly think through three sets of images from different moments in the history of photographic-based media to assess both how their sense of presence might be constructed in relation to the movement *of* the image, or of bodies *in* the image, as well as how, because of the overdetermined relation between photography and the racial body, at times the image appears unable to contain this body's seemingly overflowing presence. Each set of images also illustrates the entanglement between the legislative archive and the political ontology of the black subject (addressed as a question of movement) as it unfolds in the surrounding visual and media culture.

The first is situated at the beginning of the photographic medium and illustrates how it was immediately enlisted by the natural sciences in order to prove the *visual fact* of racial difference. In 1850, Swiss natural scientist Luis Agassiz commissioned a series of daguerreotypes of slaves in order to "scientifically" examine the "radical" differences of their physical features, thereby "proving" his theory of polygenesis, that is, the idea that human races were distinct species and organized according to one Great Chain of Being, which regarded Africans as the missing link between primates and Europeans. The daguerreotypes that Joseph T. Zealy took in Columbia, South Carolina, on Agassiz's behalf allowed the scientist to study, in the comfort of Harvard University's facilities, the body of individuals who would have no longer been slaves if they had been examined in the free state of Massachusetts. Agassiz had visited several plantations in South Carolina to identify the individuals he wanted to study, but the daguerreotypes proved more expedient: they both "captured" and "released" the (image of the) slaves. They fixated the slaves' image and thus reproduced their captivity in photographic form—a fixation that they had to cooperate with, given that the technology of the daguerreotype required them to stand still for over a minute. Yet, while this photographic reproduction afforded their stillness—their visual existence as specimens for his clinical gaze—it also assured their (image's) portability, that is, their transportation to a place they could have not gone to otherwise, so that the scientist could perform his observations without having to take an explicit stand on the question of slavery, or be in the actual presence of the slaves.[86]

The second example takes place at the beginning of cinema and it involves Jack Johnson, the first black heavyweight champion of the world. Johnson was an overpowering boxer in the ring and a defiantly independent personality and notoriously controversial figure, particularly due to his association with white women. He enjoyed phenomenal mobility in social, racial, and physical terms. Because of this, Johnson was at the center of a legislative effort to contain him. First, this effort worked to contain his movement across racial lines: his association with white women triggered the passage of the 1910 Mann Act banning "white slavery," which prohibited the transportation of unmarried white women across state borders. Second, the effort to stop his physical mobility extended to the investment in preventing the circulation of *images* of his movements *as a boxer*. This prompted the passage of the 1912 Sims Act banning the interstate commerce of fight films, a measure intended to stop the circulation of footage of his victories over white opponents, in particular his 1910 victory over Jim Jeffries, who was urged out of retirement to fight Johnson and keep the title within the white race.

In arguing in favor of the ability of state censorship boards to prevent the circulation and exhibition of Jack Johnson's fight films on grounds of immorality, pressure groups would claim "we don't want Jack Johnson in this part of the country," thus treating the films as *equivalents* of Johnson's actual physical presence. In other words, a moving image of his moving body *counted as* the actual presence of his moving body.[87] This ban on interstate circulation of immoral materials was made possible by the fact that, at the time, films were still conceptualized as items of commerce—like any other commodity object—rather than as cultural expressions, which could be protected by the constitutional guarantee of free speech. As such, the footage could only move as a physical object—rolls of film in a can—and was thus subject to the same challenge that any kind of smuggling would have to face—almost. In 1914, Johnson lost his title against Jess Willard in a fight in Havana, Cuba, and there was great public demand to see the film. The producer, Lawrence Weber, devised a way around the ban, making sure that the footage, which had been developed in Toronto, could enter the United States. He organized a projection of the film into the United States from the Canadian side of the border so that it could be rephotographed on the US side. Even though the film *moved* without physical movement, the existence of a reconstituted "film object" in the United States triggered yet another legislative response, extending the attempt to control Johnson's physical movement to the movement of the rays of light that had "carried" the film across the border.

This effort to stop the visual record of Johnson's body in order to stop the body itself discloses the very distinction between the two that it is also disavows. What is it about the image of a black body that makes the body feel present in the same space as its viewer? The sight of a black body moving effectively, purposefully, and efficiently—within a young medium that has the unique ability to deliver moving pictures—is central to the unbearable sense of the body's actual presence. Unfolding in the cinematic mode of presence, Johnson's moving body created an effect of *liveness* that threatened to overcome the very thing that mediated images cannot achieve: the copresence of seer and seen in the same space.

The judicial use of George Holliday's video of the beating of Rodney King produced, in part, a similar sense of presence. In this footage, the body's movement is of a different kind. King is not moving by his volition but rather in reaction to the baton strikes inflicted upon him. Scholarship on the video has always begun from the observation that, when seen in its entirety, the way it was broadcast on national TV, the video offered unmistakable evidence of the violence inflicted on King. Yet, when the video entered the Simi Valley courtroom, the attorneys for the police officers argued that its evidence could only be decoded by expert testimony. Speaking to the video and sometimes touching selected moments and areas of the screen image, St. Duke, the expert witness, argued that the officers' actions followed appropriate professional protocols; he thus offered a justification for every single baton strike against an already subdued Rodney King. In the courtroom, the video is arrested and fragmented into smaller units, and, in this frame-by-frame analysis, King's bodily movements become similar to those of a wind-up doll. This new, reedited, "mechanical body" can be represented as non-sentient, and yet, contradictorily, still a threat. The "presence" of King's body in the video is powerful enough to tap into the fear of the aggressively moving black body, while the presence/fact/ reality of King's body *in pain* does not come through. Within this highly selective sense of presence, the body's twitching under the blows of police batons is reread as still possessing an offensive agency that needs to be tamed.

As Elizabeth Alexander articulates in her influential essay, "Can you be Black and Look at This?" there is a bodily archive of practical memory that is reactivated at the moment of collective spectatorship of the black body in pain.[88] In this (visual) connection to the past, "the black body" remembers what has been done to it. The implication is that the image remembers as well because of the way it has accumulated a history of past ways of framing the black body that rarely allow it to come through as a sentient living subject, and, even less, as unbound and full of potential. Yet there is nothing in photographic ontology as such—that is, considered in isolation from race—that can explain this fact.

Each of these examples shows that the image can be available for something other than mimesis, captivity, scientific or juridical study, or presence, and it can perform many types of cultural work. The image can disclose the continued callous tolerance for black pain, as in the case of the Rodney King video and the many others that have followed in the past two years alone (Eric Garner, Walter Scott, Tamir Rice, etc.); it can be a conduit for collective mourning, as in the case of *Fruitvale Station*, which is built around the footage of the shooting of Oscar Grant; it can be a space of agency and mobility for a black body unbound by social constraints, as in the case of Jack Johnson's fight films; and it can function as a philosophical toy, a thinking thing, as in the case of Spike Lee's *Bamboozled*.

Notes

1   See Brandi Wilkins Catanese, *The Problem of the Color [blind]: Racial Transgression and the Politics of Black Performance* (Ann Harbor: University of Michigan Press, 2011).

2   Neil Gotanda, "A Critique of 'Our Constitution Is Color-Blind,'" in *Critical Race Theory: The Key Writings that Formed the Movement*, ed. Kimberlé Crenshaw, Neil Gotanda, Gary Peller, and Kendall Thomas (New York: New Press, 1995), 257–75. "Status race" was upheld in the 1857 Supreme Court decision *Dred Scott v. Sandford*, the case that claimed that the Constitution excludes "Negroes" from the orbit of protection it extends to citizens.

3 W. J. T. Mitchell asks how we need to understand "race" in order to continue to criticize racism. The title of his book—*Seeing through Race* (Cambridge, MA: Harvard University Press, 2012)—is deliberately ambiguous: is race something we have already *seen through* and ultimately dismissed? Has race become invisible, or does it continue to provide a lens, framework, or medium for the distribution of power, subjectivity, and humanity?

4 Stephen Best, *The Fugitive's Properties, Law and the Poetics of Possession* (Chicago and London: University of Chicago Press, 2004), 81. Unlike the slave, whose model of personhood it adopts, the corporate person is immediately born privileged and, to some extent, amoral: the corporation has "personality (but not a face), intentions (but no feelings), relationships (but no family or friends), responsibility (but no conscience), and susceptibility to punishment (but no capacity for pain)." Elizabeth Hankins Wolgast, *Ethics of an Artificial Person: Lost Responsibility in Professions and Organizations* (Stanford, CA: Stanford University Press, 1992), 86.

5 Richard Dyer, *White* (London: Routledge, 1997).

6 Shawn Michelle Smith, *Photography on the Color Line: W.E.B. Du Bois, Race, and Visual Culture* (Durham, NC: Duke University Press, 2004).

7 W. E. B. Du Bois, *Souls of Black Folk* (New York: Library of America, 1990), 8.

8 Frantz Fanon, *Black Skins, White Masks*, trans. Richard Philcox (New York: Grove Press, 2008), 92.

9 Jacques Lacan, "The Mirror Stage as Formative of the *I* Function," in *Écrits: The First Complete Edition in English*, trans. Bruce Fink (New York: Norton, 2006), 75–81.

10 Diana Fuss, "Interior Colonies: Frantz Fanon and the Politics of Identification," *Diacritics* 24, nos 2–3 (1994): 19–42; Smith, *Photography on the Color Line*, Ch. 1.

11 Maurice Merleau-Ponty, *Phenomenology of Perception*, trans. Colin Smith (London: Routledge, 1962).

12 Sic. Charles Johnson, "A Phenomenology of the Black Body," *Michigan Quarterly Review* 32, no. 4 (1993): 606.

13 Harvey Young, *Embodying Black Experience: Stillness, Critical Memory, and the Black Body* (Ann Arbor: University of Michigan Press, 2010), 1–25.

14 Stuart Hall, "The After-Life of Frantz Fanon: Why Fanon? Why Now? Why *Black Skins, White Masks?*," in *The Fact of Blackness: Frantz Fanon and Visual Representation*, ed. Alan Read (Seattle, WA: Bay Press, 1996), 20.

15 Kobena Mercer, "Busy in the Ruins of a Wretched Phantasia," in *Frantz Fanon: Critical Perspectives*, ed. Anthony Alessandrini (London and New York: Routledge, 1999), 28; Michele Wallace, "Afterword: 'Why Are There No Great Black Artists?': The Problem of Visuality in African-American Culture," in *Black Popular Culture*, ed. Gina Dent (Seattle, WA: Bay Press, 1992).

16 Justice Henry Billings Brown, "Majority Opinion in *Plessy v. Ferguson*," in *Desegregation and the Supreme Court*, ed. Benjamin Munn Ziegler (Boston: D. C. Heath and Company, 1958), 50–51. The hermeneutic effort of "detecting" race did not diminish the desire to establish clear, biological boundaries; eventually, it was the visual confusion of the passing subject that prompted various US states to pass legislation that continued to locate racial identity in blood, with the "one drop rule."

17 Best, *The Fugitive's Properties*, 203–67.

18 Cited in Mark Elliot, "Race, Color Blindness, and the Democratic Public: Albion W. Tourgee's Radical Principles in Plessy V. Ferguson," *The Journal of Southern History* 67 (2001): 288.

19 Amy Robinson, "Forms of Appearance of Value: Homer Plessy and the Politics of Privacy," in *Performance and Cultural Politics*, ed. Elin Diamond (London and New York: Routledge, 1996), 237–61; Cheryl Harris, "Whiteness as Property," in *Critical Race Theory: The Key Writings that Formed the Movement*, ed. Kimberlé Crenshaw, Neil Gotanda, Gary Peller, and Kendall Thomas (New York: New Press, 1995), 276–91.

20 Mark Golub, "Plessy as 'Passing': Judicial Responses to Ambiguously Raced Bodies in Plessy V. Ferguson," *Law & Society Review* 39, no. 3 (2005): 563–600.

21 Robyn Wiegman, *American Anatomies: Theorizing Race and Gender* (Durham, NC, and London: Duke University Press,

1995); Michele Foucault, *Discipline and Punish: The Birth of the Prison* (New York: Vintage, 1979).

22 Elizabeth Abel, "Bathroom Doors and Drinking Fountains," *Critical Inquiry* 25 (1999): 451.

23 Best, *The Fugitive's Properties*, 203–67; Jacquelyn Stewart, *Migrating to the Movies Cinema and Black Urban Modernity* (Berkeley: University of California Press, 2005); Jane Gaines, *Fire and Desire: Mixed-Race Movies in the Silent Era* (Chicago: University of Chicago Press, 2001); Lynne Kirby, *Parallel Tracks: The Railroad and Silent Cinema* (Durham, NC: Duke University Press, 1997); Alice Maurice, *The Cinema and Its Shadow: Race and Technology in Early Cinema* (Minneapolis: University of Minnesota Press, 2013); Susan Courtney, *Hollywood's Fantasies of Miscegenation: Spectacular Narratives of Gender and Race, 1903–1967* (Princeton and Oxford: Princeton University Press, 2005).

24 Anna Everett, *Returning the Gaze: A Genealogy of Black Film Criticism, 1909–1949* (Durham, NC, and London: Duke University Press, 2001); Lauren Berlant, "National Brands/ National Body: *Imitation of Life*," in *Comparative American Identities: Race, Sex, and Nationality in the Modern Text*, ed. Hortense J. Spillers (New York and London: Routledge, 1991), 110–40; Doris Witt, *Black Hunger: Food and the Politics of U.S. Identity* (New York and Oxford: Oxford University Press, 1999).

25 Courtney, *Hollywood's Fantasies of Miscegenation*, 147.

26 Rosemary Coombe, *The Cultural Life of Intellectual Properties: Authorship, Appropriation and the Law* (Durham, NC: Duke University Press, 1998).

27 The passage from Marx's *Capital* where he presents his theory of commodity fetishism is often referred to as the "dancing table."

28 Michael Schudson, "Advertising as Capitalist Realism," *Advertising & Society Review* 1, no. 1 (2000), *Project MUSE*, April 11, 2016, https://muse.jhu.edu/. Accessed on June 20, 2015.

29 Mark Smith, *How Race Is Made: Slavery, Segregation, and the Senses* (Chapel Hill: University of North Carolina Press, 2006).

30 Julia Kristeva, *The Powers of Horror: An Essay on Abjection* (New York: Columbia University Press, 1982), 4. See also

Kathryn Bond Stockton, *Beautiful Bottom, Beautiful Shame: Where "Black" Meets "Queer"* (Durham, NC: Duke University Press, 2006). Lee Daniels' film *Precious* (2009) is often discussed in terms of abjection. See special issue of *Black Camera* 4, no. 1 (2012).

31 Fanon, *Black Skins,* 93.

32 Ibid., 96 and 102.

33 Johnson, "Phenomenology of the Black Body," 606.

34 Frantz Fanon, *Wretched of the Earth* (New York: Grove Press, 1963), 52; Darieck Scott, *Extravagant Abjection: Blackness, Power, and Sexuality in the African American Literary Imagination* (New York: NYU Press, 2010). Scott discusses these concepts under the heading "Fanon's muscles."

35 James Snead, "Repetition as a Figure of Black Culture," in *Black Literature and Literary Theory*, ed. Henry Louis Gates (New York and London: Methuen, 1984), 59–80.

36 Kara Keeling, "In the Interval: Frantz Fanon and the 'Problems' of Visual Representation," *Qui Parle* 13, no. 2 (2003): 101.

37 bell hooks, "Eating the Other," in *Black Looks: Race and Representation* (Boston and New York: South End Press, 1992).

38 See Danielle Allen, *Talking to Strangers: Anxieties of Citizenship after Brown v. Board of Education* (Chicago: University of Chicago Press, 2004).

39 Mercer, "Busy," 202. Or, as James Baldwin explained, the object of one's hatred is never located conveniently outside, but rather it is "seated in one's lap, stirring in one's bowels and dictating the beating of one's heart." James Baldwin, *The Price of the Ticket: Collected Nonfiction 1948–1985* (New York: St. Martin's Press), 686.

40 Anne Anlin Cheng, *The Melancholy of Race: Psychoanalysis, Assimilation and Hidden Grief* (Oxford University Press, 2000).

41 Several paradoxes overlap. First, the protagonist is "invisible" because he is hypervisible. Second, the mark of invisibility (i.e., his blackness) is a visible mark. Third, to be seen is to be recognized as the unrecognizable or as a transparent vessel. Ralph Ellison, *Invisible Man* (New York: Vintage Books, 1995).

42 Sharon Holland, *The Erotic Life of Racism* (Durham, NC: Duke University Press, 2012), 41. Holland rephrases a question posed

by philosopher Emmanuel Levinas. For Holland, desire is always interlaced with race.

43 See Christina Sharpe, *Monstrous Intimacies: Making Post-Slavery Subjects* (Durham, NC: Duke University Press, 2010); Tavia Nyong'o, *The Amalgamation Waltz: Race, Performance, and the Ruses of Memory* (Minneapolis: University of Minnesota Press, 2009).

44 Kimberly Benston, "I Yam What I Am: The Topos of Un(Naming) in Afro-American Literature," in *Black Literature and Literary Theory*, ed. Henry Louis Gates (New York and London: Methuen, 1984), 151–72.

45 Henry Louis Gates, *The Signifying Monkey: A Theory of African-American Literary Criticism* (New York: Oxford University Press, 1988). The concept of the performativity of race comes from the application of Judith Butler's ideas about gender as performance.

46 Patrick Johnson, *Appropriating Blackness: Performance and the Politics of Authenticity* (Durham, NC: Duke University Press, 2003). See also Debbie Thompson, "'Is Race a Trope?': Anna Deavere Smith and the Question of Racial Performativity," *African American Review* 37, no. 1 (2003): 127–38; Daphne Brooks, *Bodies in Dissent. Spectacular Performances of Race and Freedom, 1850–1910* (Durham and London: Duke University Press, 2006) and Thomas F. DeFrantz and Anita Gonzalez, eds, *Black Performance Theory* (Durham, NC, and London: Duke University Press, 2014).

47 Fanon, *Black Skins*, 89.

48 Robin Bernstein, "Dances with Things: Material Culture and the Performance of Race," *Social Text* 27, no. 4 (2009): 67–94.

49 Fanon, *Black Skins*, 90–91.

50 Sara Ahmed, "The Phenomenology of Whiteness," *Feminist Theory* 8, no. 2 (2007): 149–68. Ultimately the immediate, natural, unthinking gesture responsible for the death of Oscar Grant caught on camera and featured at the beginning of *Fruitvale Station* (Ryan Coogler, 2013) is an appalling but vivid example of white orientation.

51 Tavia Nyong'o, "Racial Kitsch and Black Performance," *The Yale Journal of Criticism* 15, no. 2 (2002): 216.

52 Huey Copeland, *Bound to Appear: Art, Slavery, and the Site of Blackness in Multicultural America* (Chicago: University of Chicago Press, 2013).

53 Hortense J. Spillers, "Mama's Baby, Papa's Maybe: An American Grammar Book," *Diacritics* 17, no. 2 (1987): 65–81. See also Alexander Weheliye, *Habeas Viscus: Racializing Assemblages, Biopolitics and Black Feminist Theories of the Human* (Durham, NC: Duke University Press, 2014).

54 Such ideas occur in theoretical frameworks that fall under the rubrics of Object-Oriented Ontology, Speculative Realism, and New Materialism, for example.

55 Martin Heidegger, *Being and Time*, trans. Joan Stambaugh and Dennis J. Schmidt (New York: SUNY Press, 2010).

56 Saidiya Hartman, *Scenes of Subjection: Terror, Slavery, and Self-Making in Nineteenth-Century America* (New York: Oxford University Press, 1997), 24.

57 Ian Baucom, *Specters of the Atlantic: Finance Capital, Slavery, and the Philosophy of History* (Durham, NC, and London: Duke University Press, 2005).

58 Jacques Derrida, *Specters of Marx: The State of Debt, the Work of Mourning, and the New International*, trans. Peggy Kamuf (New York and London: Routledge, 2006).

59 John Akomfrah, "Digitopia and the Spectres of Diaspora," *Journal of Media Practice* 11, no. 1 (2010): 21–29.

60 Marcus Wood, *Blind Memory: Visual Representations of Slavery in England and America 1780–1865* (New York: Routledge, 2000).

61 From a ship ledger found in the *Book Negro*, cited by Katherine McKittrick, "Mathematics Black Life," *The Black Scholar* 44, no. 2 (2014): 17. See Saidiya Hartman, "Venus in Two Acts," *Small Axe* 26 (2008): 1–14.

62 I am following Jennifer C. Nash's assessment of what she calls the "black feminist archive": Jennifer Nash, *The Black Body in Ecstasy* (Durham, NC: Duke University Press, 2014).

63 As Shohat and Stam summarized this point, "On the symbolic battlegrounds of the mass media, the struggle over representation in the simulacral realm *homologizes* that of the

political sphere, where questions of imitation and representation easily slide into issues of delegation and voice." Ella Shohat and Robert Stam, *Unthinking Eurocentrism: Multiculturalism and the Media* (London and New York: Routledge, 1994), 183 (my emphasis). The fundamental text on the question of the two meanings of representation is Gayatri Spivak, "Can the Subaltern Speak?," in *Marxism and the Interpretation of Culture*, ed. C. Nelson and Lawrence Grossberg (Basingstoke: Macmillan Education, 1988), 271–313.

64 Homi Bhabha, "Of Mimicry and Men," *The Location of Culture* (London and New York: Routledge, 1994).

65 Fanon, *Black Skins*, 140.

66 Keeling, "In the Interval." See also David Marriott, "Waiting to Fall," *CR: The New Centennial Review* 13, no. 3 (2013): 163–240.

67 Toni Morrison, *Playing in the Dark: Whiteness and the Literary Imagination* (New York: Vintage Books, 1992), xi.

68 W. J. T. Mitchell, *What Do Pictures Want? The Lives and Loves of Images* (Chicago and London: University of Chicago Press, 2005), 298.

69 Stuart Hall, "What Is This 'Black' in Black Popular Culture?," in *Black Popular Culture*, ed. Gina Dent (Seattle, WA: Bay Press, 1992), 32.

70 Homi Bhabha, "The Other Question," *The Location of Culture* (London and New York: Routledge, 1994).

71 Kobena Mercer, "Skin Head Sex Thing: Racial Difference and the Homoerotic Imaginary," in *How Do I Look? Queer Film and Video*, ed. Bad Object-Choices (Seattle, WA: Bay Press, 1991), 177.

72 Ibid., 207.

73 Gwendolyn DuBois Shaw, *Seeing the Unspeakable: The Art of Kara Walker* (Durham, NC: Duke University Press, 2004); Howardena Pindell, *Kara Walker-No, Kara Walker-Yes, Kara Walker-?* (New York: Midmarch Arts Press, 2009) and Alessandra Raengo, "Life in Those Shadows! Kara Walker's Post-cinematic Silhouettes," in *Post-Cinema: Theorizing 21st-Century Film*, ed. Julia Leyda and Shane Denson (REFRAME Books, 2016). http://reframe.sussex.ac.uk/post-cinema/5-5-raengo/. Accessed on April 15, 2016.

74 The controversial poster for the film, which the *New York Times* refused to run as an ad, was inspired by Charles's work. Some of the figurines come from his personal collection, while others belong to Spike Lee.

75 Manthia Diawara, "The Blackface Stereotype," introduction to David Levinthal, *Blackface* (Santa Fe, NM: Arena Editions, 1999), 7 and 9.

76 The political economy of the sign describes the way Jean Baudrillard has read Marx's concept of the political economy of capital, whereby the signifier corresponds to the commodity's exchange value and the signified to its use-value. Jean Baudrillard, *For a Critique of the Political Economy of the Sign* (St. Louis: Telos Press, 1981).

77 Eric Lott, *Love and Theft: Blackface Minstrelsy and the American Working Class* (New York: Oxford University Press, 1993), 18–19. The account that Eric Lott uses is derived from an *Atlantic Monthly* article from 1867.

78 Ralph Ellison, "Change the Joke and Slip the Yoke," in *The Collected Essays of Ralph Ellison*, 100–12 (New York: Modern Library Edition, 1995), 107 (my emphasis).

79 Michael Rogin, *Blackface, White Noise: Jewish Immigrants in the Hollywood Melting Pot* (Berkeley: University of California Press, 1996), 14 (my emphasis). The transformative moments—moments that combine box office success, critical recognition of revolutionary significance, formal innovations, and shifts in the cinematic mode of production—are the beginning of cinema (he cites Edwin Porter's *Uncle Tom's Cabin*, 1903), the beginning of classical cinema (D. W. Griffith's *Birth of a Nation*, 1915), the transition to sound (*The Jazz Singer*, Alan Crosland, 1927), and the beginning of the unit mode of production (*Gone With the Wind*, Victor Fleming, 1939).

80 Meghan Sutherland, "Populism and Spectacle," *Cultural Studies* 26, nos 2–3 (2012): 339. Her references are Ernesto Laclau's concept of the people and Guy Debord's notion of spectacle.

81 Fanon, *Black Skins*, 89 (my emphasis).

82 Nicole R. Fleetwood, *Troubling Vision: Performance, Visuality, and Blackness* (Chicago: University of Chicago Press, 2011).

83 Coco Fusco, "Racial Time, Racial Marks, Racial Metaphors," in *Only Skin Deep: Changing Visions of the American Self*, ed. Brian Wallis Coco Fusco (New York: International Center of Photography, 2003). In her introduction to this historic exhibition catalogue Fusco explains the implication between photography and racialization with a reference to the visual culture repercussions of the *Plessy* decision, which insisted that the races had to remain separate so long as they were distinguishable by color.

84 Peter Wollen read Andre Bazin's essay, "The Ontology of the Photographic Image" (in *What is Cinema? Vol. 1*, trans. Hugh Gray [Berkeley: University of California Press, 1967]) as fundamentally arguing for the indexicality of photography. For many years, much of film studies followed this reading and considered photographic truth as a consequence of photography's semiotic structure—that is, beyond iconically resembling the object it records, photography is also materially connected to it, as an indexical sign. Peter Wollen, *Signs and Meaning in the Cinema* (Bloomington: University of Indiana Press, 1969). See also Roland Barthes, *Camera Lucida* (New York: Hill and Wang, 1981); and Herve Joubert-Laurencing and Dudley Andrew, eds, *Opening Bazin: Postwar Film Theory and Its Afterlife* (Oxford: Oxford University Press, 2011), for a critique of this paradigm.

85 Jean-Louis Comolli, "Machines of the Visible," in *The Cinematic Apparatus*, ed. Stephen Heath and Teresa de Lauretis (New York: St. Martin's Press, 1980).

86 Young, *Embodying Black Experience*, 26–50.

87 See Lee Grieveson, "Fighting Films: Race, Morality, and the Governing of Cinema, 1912–1915," *Cinema Journal* 38, no. 1 (1998): 40–72.

88 Elizabeth Alexander, "Can You Be Black and Look at This?," *Public Culture* 7, no. 1 (1994): 77–94.

CHAPTER TWO

Critical Race Theory and *Bamboozled*

Bamboozled is a satire of the desire for blackness in American mass media. It centers on a television writer, Pierre Delacroix, who is so dissatisfied with his inability to bring to production successful shows with "positive content" about the black middle class that he decides to write a satirical minstrel show in the hope that the outrage caused would get him fired. Unexpectedly, however, the show he conceptualizes and develops with his assistant Sloan, called *Mantan: The New Millennium Minstrel Show*, is a tremendous success, and it unleashes a widespread blackface mania among audiences now finally given license to work out their fetishization of blackness.

Delacroix, played by Damon Wayans, works for a fictional network called CNS. To offset declining viewership, his immediate superior, the producer Thomas Dunwitty (played by Michael Rappaport) puts Delacroix in charge of writing the gutsy black show that will turn the network's fortunes around. Sloan Hopkins (Jada Pinkett Smith) helps him in this endeavor and supports his choice to employ two street performers—Manray and Womack, played by tap dancer Savion Glover and stand-up comedian Tommy Davidson, respectively—as the show's stars. Yet, she becomes increasingly critical of Delacroix's artistic decisions, as she realizes his intention to revive the stereotypical cast of characters of the traditional minstrel show and disapproves of his demand that the performers wear the traditional blackface. Once the show is successfully pitched to Dunwitty, who is immediately aroused by the idea, and quickly produced and brought on air, Sloan becomes entirely powerless to stop the blackface mania that ensues. While the entire country is gripped by blackface, a group of self-defined militant gangsta rappers called The Mau Maus, led by Sloan's brother Julius (who renames himself Big Blak Afrika and is played by Mos Def), resolves to take action against the show. Eventually, the group decides to kidnap Manray, the star of the show, and execute him. His death triggers a series of other deaths (the Mau Maus themselves are killed by the police during a raid of their hideout, and then Delacroix himself is shot by a distraught Sloan) as the film transitions away from satire and into a more properly tragic generic framework, whereupon the audience discovers that Delacroix's narration might have been posthumous the entire time. The film ends with Delacroix's slow death, which ushers in a montage of racist media images from film and television history, while Delacroix's voiceover repeats the admonition of his father Junebug (who is a stand-up comedian played by Paul Mooney): "always keep 'em laughing."

The ostensible theme of the film is the question of representation and, in Lee's own words, "the power of images," that is, the social impact that media images can have in general, and not simply in relation to race.[1] Yet, the film is also highly reflexive; it is a film about a TV show that features a minstrel show. The film employs a nontraditional approach to these issues, and, through a series of moves, it dismantles the very logic that sustains both the stereotype and the request for positive representations. It does so by creating a deluge of stereotypical and troubling images that appear to have no clear referent in the real world. Time and time again, scholarly responses to the film highlight how this barrage of demeaning images conveys the unattainability of a stable black identity in postmodern times, raising difficult questions about the ownership and self-definition of blackness and about the authenticity of black representations.

Bamboozled was not very popular at the box office, but it has enjoyed tremendous critical success. It is a densely theoretical film that has contributed to a variety of theoretical approaches, including theories of representation, communication, rhetoric, mass media and mass culture, material and visual culture, the popular, performance, masquerade, passing, signifyin(g), commodification, exploitation, reification, abjection, racial grotesque, the uncanny, post-humanism, and hauntology, among others.[2]

The film is indeed about representations in popular culture, but, rather than endorsing or even seeking their authenticity, it investigates the process that Stuart Hall has emphasized— the fact that "the popular" has the ability to fix mass cultural forms, with blackness in particular holding the capacity to reify these forms, even while it continues to display an enormous fluidity and fungibility. Thus, it is important to keep in mind that the film is assembled in the spirit of archival and curatorial practice; hence it purposefully functions as a capacious container for a tremendous amount of racist imagery. All the while, it maintains a complex melancholic relation with the materials it contains, including samples from the "art of the stereotype" discussed earlier, as well as a number of clips from film and television history.

In its investigation of multiple processes of reification—that is, images becoming things, stereotypes becoming masks, blackface becoming mechanical objects—*Bamboozled* structures itself as one of these objects: a wind-up (philosophical) toy propelled by the desire of its multiple internal and external audiences. Movement, whether self-directed or initiated, demanded or coerced, is key to the way the film thinks about the relationship between the Black and the human. Thus, I have organized the following analysis in a way that adheres to this structure so that, by the end, one might discover having been moved by the very object that one has been moving all along.

Where's Waldo? Finding the stereotype

The vast majority of scholarly readings of the film begin by expressing dissatisfaction with the way *Bamboozled* handles the question of representation. Thus, these readings feature a long litany of stereotypes—not only the stereotypes that the media industry circulates but also, more shockingly, the stereotypes that the film deliberately engenders for virtually every single one of its characters. Often, scholars conclude with the blanket accusation that the film reinforces all these stereotypes, and, as such, it remains prisoner to this reckless accumulation of damaging images.

If one were to use the canonical book in stereotype analysis, Donald Bogle's *Toms, Coons, Mulattoes, Mammies and Bucks: An Interpretive History of Blacks in American Film*, as a checklist, one would find that *Bamboozled* contains all of Bogle's stereotypes and more. This is deliberate, and it is done to create an effect of nausea and a sense of utter predictability through the experience of the stereotypes' accumulation, even when one is often shocked to see how successful they become in the film. So, the traditional approach—whereby the critical act is spent in the pursuit of stereotypes—becomes a game of "Finding Waldo," a futile search to tease out a core of authenticity within a purposefully grotesque and excessive accumulation of demeaning images across a variety of media.

Thus, the first pedagogical exercise I propose as a way to unlock the film and at the same time see how quickly stereotypes reify, is the search for the stereotype, which will open up the many other ways in which *Bamboozled* also works.[3] Let us give it a quick try. The production of *Mantan: The New Millennium Minstrel Show* sits at the core of the film. Unsurprisingly, everything about it—from conception to production to execution and audience reaction—will unavoidably rely on stereotypical assumptions, which is one of the points that Lee wants to make: this is the workaday reality of the media industry, and, most of the time, we just pretend not to notice the industry's foundational dependence on stereotypes.

Delacroix's simple decision to revive the minstrel show—which he mildly, yet insightfully, describes as a "variety show" in order to prove his point that the industry only wants to see blacks as buffoons—implies the reanimation of very old stereotypical characters. The show's two star performers—Manray and Womack, unceremoniously renamed Mantan and Sleep 'N Eat—are marketed as "two real coons," the first of a series of throwbacks to the construction of authenticity that underlies the counterfeit nature of the minstrel show, as well as to the "reality effect" produced by the accumulation of (in this case, highly competing) signifiers: a "real" "coon." By agreeing to play the part, they come into tragic contact with the demeaning process of colluding with one's own fetishization, while they also undertake an archival journey into the experience of past entertainers and the types of negotiations these earlier performers had to manage.

The literature on the film describes the coon as a character usually deployed for comic relief who stresses his own inferiority, acting dumb and ineffective. Elements of this caricature are slack-jawed ignorance, gaping grins, and clumsy body humor. The coon stereotype trucks in buffoonish and absurdist behavior that almost always ends in debasement for the character. With this in mind, we might be able to find other "coons," who are perhaps less openly advertised—Delacroix, for example.

By his own sarcastic admission, Delacroix is an "Oreo" (black on the outside and white on the inside) and a "sellout"—or as Dunwitty puts it, a bourgeois Negro with "buppie ways" who is estranged from black culture—yet he too agrees to "coon" to please his boss. Examples occur in the scenes where he pitches his idea for the updated minstrel show and where he wins several Golden Globe awards for *Mantan*. The latter scene is a parody of two high-profile moments of celebration of black achievement in the media industry: Cuba Gooding, Jr.'s acceptance speech for his Oscar as best supporting actor in *Jerry McGuire* (Cameron Crowe, 1997) and Ving Rhames's decision to gift Jack Lemmon the 1998 Golden Globe for best actor Rhames won for his performance of Don King. Both instances showcased an unnecessary humility and servility on the part of the black performers recognized by these awards. With his parody, Lee not only highlights their seemingly uncontrollable impulse to "coon" in order to express gratitude but also reveals the way in which their actions follow the profile of the ultimately desirable black presence in Hollywood: humble, loving, generous. "If I had done that," Delacroix's voiceover comments, "I would have been assured of work forever. Delacroix, the grateful Negro."

Delacroix fits this mold in important, but not definitive, ways. He is eager to please, soft-spoken, and seemingly plays by the rules, yet his affectation, impeccable style of dress, precise grammar, and impossible diction ("Grace-Kelley-meets-James-Earl-Jones," as it has been described)[4]—emphatically showcased in the film's opening when he gives a dictionary definition of *satire* and then addresses the camera to introduce himself as a "creative person" "responsible for what you see in that 'idiot box'"—indicate from the outset how he is an egregiously fabricated and self-contained character that does not seek a clear counterpart in the real world. His own father, Junebug, cannot help but exasperatedly ask: "Nigger, where the fuck did you get that accent?" Delacroix presents both a caricature of the educated, "non-threatening African-American male"—as Dunwitty and PR specialist Myrna Goldfarb (Dina Pearlman) describe him without his objection, he "acts white"—and, unavoidably by contrast, the equally problematic association of whiteness with intellectual and high-class values *and* the corollary idea that blacks are intrinsically barred from, or impermeable, to these values. Delacroix is therefore both the embodiment of a range of stereotypical traits and a prolific producer of old and new ones.

As a blackface minstrel show, *Mantan* works as a container for an assortment of stereotypical characters originally associated with the antebellum South that, however, have survived in later media and consumer culture. For example, the program uses the Mammy, famously embodied by the Aunt Jemima figure, and her male counterpart, Rastus. The show also features various "pickaninnies," fittingly modeled after Topsy, the compulsively moving child from *Uncle Tom's Cabin*, as well as Mark Twain's Nigger Jim. As he is pitching the show to Dunwitty, Delacroix sarcastically refers to them as "fully tridimensional characters," with traits such as laziness and stupidity, which he sets out to revive in order to test the amount of desire and attachment such stereotypes can still produce. This very idea that one can revive stereotypes without consequence is precisely his most damning miscalculation, an error that then precipitates the tragic denouement of the film. Grown out of proportion, the stereotypes suffocate their own "creator," who eventually begins to hallucinate; he imagines that the blackface collectibles with which he has surrounded himself have come alive.

The point of accumulating these archetypal stereotypes is not only to highlight how obviously recognizable they are, but also to show how "common" they are, which, in this case, means both *commonsensical* and how available they are as common resources, in other words, common properties. This fact had been recognized as far back as the intellectual property case *Stowe vs. Thomas*, which failed to protect Harriet Beecher Stowe's *Uncle Tom's Cabin* from unauthorized appropriation and translation, precisely because of the commonality of the stereotypical characters she had created.[5]

While in *Do the Right Thing*, Public Enemy and their song "Fight the Power" were showcased as examples of militant rap, in *Bamboozled*, the Mau Maus, named after a Kenyan revolutionary group that fought against colonialism, offer its caricature. Outfitted as Afrocentric gangsta rappers, the self-proclaimed militant group is painfully ignorant and profoundly inarticulate about its own political stance. Despite the pseudo-revolutionary bent, the Mau Maus engage in the very behavior they seem to despise—for instance, drinking "Da Bomb" malt liquor or fancy bottled water. Even though they are rightly critical of the media industry's hunger for minstrel-type blackness, the Mau Maus audition for the *Mantan* show, don't get the part, and, when they decide to act, they misdirect their anger onto Manray, who had just come to the realization that he could no longer be complicit with the industry's requests.

The stronger critique this stereotypical approach to gangsta rap might be making is precisely the idea that it might not be much different from the "cooning" that is expected in other media genres, as well as the critique of authenticity fabricated through ideas of "street cred" and "keeping it real." Interestingly though, the Mau Maus have important aesthetic and formal functions within the film, which, I argue, override the negative spin through which they are represented.

The Mau Maus harbor a stereotype that has to do with black impersonation—the White Rapper, 1/16th Blak, played by MC SERCH. The stereotype here plays off the old "one-drop" rule as a claim for authenticity by using a specific, albeit fictional, measurement of black ancestry. His 1/16th portion of black blood justifies his belonging in the rap group but singles him out during the police raid, where he is the only one who, despite his protests, is not killed. There, once again, the rule of visual recognition trumps the ostensibly legitimizing power of blood lineage.

The more vibrant black impersonator, though—the counterpart to Delacroix's "Oreo"—is his immediate boss, the network producer Dunwitty. From the beginning, he displays an extraordinary eagerness to use "inner group" language, making conspicuous use of the N-word. His justification is twofold. First, he has a black wife and two biracial children, a fact that makes him feel entitled to a series of proprietary claims on blackness, which are parodied in a variety of ways, including his exaggerated gesturing and overenthusiastic reactions. Second, he sides with Tarantino against Spike Lee in considering "nigger" just a word, which is therefore available to whites as well as blacks. The emptiness of his claim is crystalized by the fact that the debate about legitimate uses of the N-word is ultimately couched in terms of issues of hetero- or self-representation and cultural authority and is very rarely considered as a question of vernacular culture and expressivity. It is seldom discussed in relation to the rich history of radicalization of the word that emerged in the 1960s, with political comedians such as Lenny Bruce, Dick Gregory, and later Richard Pryor. Dick Gregory, in particular, titled his 1964 autobiography *Nigger* and strategically placed the following as a subtitle: "Dear Momma, every time you hear that word, remember they are advertising my book." In the sequence of Delacroix's visit to Junebug's stand-up show, the film gestures toward this tradition and allows Delacroix to voice his perplexity toward it. He asks his father, "Why do you say that word so much?" Junebug matter-of-factly answers, "I say 'nigger' 100 times every morning. It keeps my teeth white."

Dunwitty lives a vicarious blackness through his attachments and connections to the black community and has an intense investment in black popular culture. His office is decorated with (vaguely conceived) African sculptural pieces and masks, along with giant photographs of African American sports figures including Muhammad Ali, Mike Tyson, Michael Jordan, Hank Aaron, and Kareem Abdul-Jabbar, among others. Even though it is easy to identify individual black impersonators in the film, black impersonation is ultimately the most widespread type of desire in the film, which can be seen in its entirety as an investigation into the media's widespread desire to "eat the other"—a sentiment that spreads virally, beginning with the show's premier. Rather than simply stereotypical, the "love and theft" of blackness, in the sense defined by Eric Lott, is the fundamental premise of the film.

The entertainers in *Bamboozled*—whether they are *Mantan's* two stars, the Mau Maus, or performers who appear during the casting call—all demonstrate a strong sense of rhythm and pace, which are stereotypically considered innate African American talents. It would be easy to extend this stereotypical lens to Junebug too, who, in some respects, could be seen as a Chitlin' Circuit comedian. He is dressed in an outlandish, brightly colored orange outfit and tells mostly lewd and racy jokes. Yet, as independent filmmaker Zeinabu irene Davis suggests, orange is a color the film employs to show proximity to "regular folks," thus establishing the vernacular connection more appropriate to his type of comedy and the venues where he performs.[6] More importantly, Junebug is arguably the most articulate character in the film and he defies the assumption of mindless movement that accompanies the stereotype of the rhythmically inclined Black performer. Building on this assumption, he intelligently, if provocatively and matter-of-factly, states: "Every nigger is an entertainer." He is also the most liberated character and the only one who has not compromised his integrity as an artist— "I can't do the Hollywood stuff," he explains to his son, while framed in front of his reflection in a backstage mirror after his comedy act, "I can't say the stuff they want me to say." He can speak freely of the problematic tension between desire and rejection of blackness: "Everybody wanna be black, but nobody wanna be black," he says and further elaborates in his act: "They'd do anything to get big nigger lips," conjuring up a grotesque quasi-cannibalistic scenario in which "black people'd be killed on the highway—white folks come around . . . yeah, I'll take that. [. . .] They lips so big the little kids look adopted." Even though he clearly recognizes how the media capitalize on this desire for blackness—"My favorite black show is *COPS*," he says—he still struggles to explain this obsession with blackness and how to cope with the way it is still coupled with disdain for black people: "I hope they start hanging niggers again so we'll find out who's really black," he (logically, albeit provocatively) concludes.

In his comedy, Junebug revisits one of the stereotypes that inhabit the subtext of the film, that of the Buck as the epitome of sexual prowess. Playing on the myth of the black macho, he tells a street joke about the desire of a group of nuns for an escaped black mental patient who shows up buck naked at their doorsteps. The Buck resurfaces also in Junebug's appreciation for *Jerry Springer* as the all-American show: "Where else do you see three white women fighting over one nigger? With one tooth. And no job . . . And speaks fluent Ebonics . . . 'Reggie, how come you get three women?' 'They like dick, Jerry, they like dick.'" This underlying desirability of blackness—understood at minimum as a form of access to unrestrained sexuality, a form of the eroticism of the everyday—sustains the success of *Mantan: The New Millennium Minstrel Show*, but it also emerges in the TV commercials that frame the show's premiere. The "Buck," for example, is explicitly evoked in the commercial for "Da Bomb," a drink designed by black scientists as the black version of Viagra.

Due to the film's commitment to the logic of accumulation as well as its archival impulse, the most egregious stereotypes are reproduced in the blackface artifacts that appear in the film. In other words, virtually every character in *Mantan: The New Millennium Minstrel Show* has its counterpart in one of the blackface figurines. Here again, a purely exemplary, and yet not exhaustive, list might help appreciate how accretion is a deliberate strategy in the film. Among the collectibles Delacroix amasses, we can identify, at the very least, Rastus and Aunt Jemima Cookie jars; Jemima and Uncle Ben figurines (possibly salt and pepper shakers); a jig-dancing negro (hit the plank and the figure "dances"); black lantern jockeys of various sizes; a large Sambo figure and a large slave child with hands out, both with big grins and moving eyes; several statues of seated figures, sitting atop bales of cotton or large watermelons; dancing figurines; a basketball player figurine sharing many of the features of the other artifacts; and, finally, the "Jolly Nigger" bank, which "reanimates" in the scene of the "revenge of the black memorabilia," when Delacroix hallucinates about seeing the cast-iron figurine moving by itself. This deluge of stereotypes can be seen as a counterpart to the racial slurs montage sequence in *Do the Right Thing*, which offered a zero-degree representation of the racial "id," a bottom-line form of communication where nothing is being censored, repressed, redirected, or held back.[7] Lee here takes on the task not of investigating collective outrage or racial hatred, but rather a collective attachment to what blackness can unleash.

It would be easy to repeat, and therefore add to, the litany of stereotypes identified in much of the critical literature on the film. By doing that, we would be giving in to the desire of the stereotype to always be animated by our investment in it. Because the logic of the stereotype is to function as a receptacle of desire—a type of "energy" it leverages to circulate, reproduce itself, and come alive—our own critical action would allow it to "plaster" itself onto its supposed "model," continuing to accumulate density, thickness, and materiality. This list, therefore, would feed the same dynamic of desire that the film creates in order to expose and criticize it by following it through to its most dramatic consequences, where there is no longer an "outside" from which to speak.

Here is an example: overwhelmingly, the portrayal of Sloan has been criticized for embodying the stereotype of the woman who cannot get to the top without sleeping her way there. Yet, the film makes clear that this is the image of her that Delacroix is attempting to paint—it is an image she resists—thus calling into question where the film really falls on this issue. More importantly, the identification of her "stereotypical" traits might further confine the ability for her character to be and act *otherwise*; she would not have been locked into this image if it hadn't been evoked by Delacroix, and we wouldn't be discussing her failure to escape it if we weren't so convinced that this stereotype applies to her. This is to say that, with a film like *Bamboozled* that so directly and deliberately investigates the ambivalence and desire that fuels stereotypicality, the game of identification—"Where's Waldo?"—is simply not enough.

Like a runaway train

The montage sequence that captures the sweeping success of the *The New Millennium Minstrel Show* (so complete and overwhelming that it "takes off like a runaway train"[8]) is introduced by Delacroix's voiceover—"When American people want something, they want it big; they want it now"—as we see a series of swirling commodities that in the recent past have captured the fantasies of the nation: hula hoops (which appear to set the sequence in motion), beany babies, Pokémon, and the adorable pet rocks. Now, instead, the fad is "blackface, blackface, blackface!" as we see children trick-or-treating with blackface masks on. The sequence moves very quickly and toward an increasing degree of absurdity; it proceeds according to a logic of accumulation, as if mimicking the very viral spread, not only of the stereotypes that are licensed by blackface minstrelsy, but also of the very adoption of blackface itself.

One of the biggest criticisms lodged against the film is that it unleashes an imagery it cannot contain. Stereotypes are pervasive, prolific, and viral, and these should be good enough reasons not to revive them. Why create such a suffocating *deluge* of images? Furthermore, when this very impossibility of moving outside the image is interpreted as moral confusion, the question of representation is entirely reduced to a moral choice because representation is (illegitimately) considered a form of direct action. As Stanley Crouch puts it, "If you create a demeaning image of a group of people, or if you decide to earn your living through these demeaning images, you're making a moral choice. *Just like selling crack*."[9] But is that so?

Alongside the burden of representation, Spike Lee is charged with the burden of expected agency: the idea that the images he produces count as actions and that he is cunningly manipulating them. But, maybe if there is an "action" at the heart of the stereotype, it should be sought elsewhere, in the way stereotypes are moved by viewers' desires across the various narrative frames employed in the film's *mise-en-abyme* structure, that is, its show-within-show organization and the concentric narrative frames built around a performance (*Mantan*, obviously, but also Manray and Womack's street act, the casting call, Junebug's act, the Mau Maus, the commercials, and so on) and an audience (street audience, studio audience, television audience at home, audience for the casting call, and so on). The purpose of this structure is to create the effect of a hall of mirrors, whereby representations multiply seemingly indefinitely and make it difficult to determine whether we are looking at an image or its reflection. The effect is to deflect and defer the question of authenticity. This structure also affords more emphasis on the various performances embedded in the film, thus vividly underscoring the performativity of blackness and *Bamboozled*'s aggressively antiessentialist stance.

To investigate what really sets these images in motion, *Bamboozled* focuses on both sides of the ambivalence of the stereotype. On one hand, Lee exposes the virality of these images/things by multiplying them, stacking them, and by deploying blackface as a general hermeneutic of the visual surface. On the other hand, he focuses on their fixity and the active investment that goes into making and maintaining them. This explains the dominance of the mechanical object in the film and the experience of repetition in the way the object encourages a ritualistic dance around it—a repertoire of quotidian gestures and interactions with its mechanisms. With this double focus, *Bamboozled* achieves an unprecedented clarity about how much stereotypes are built and animated by desire.

One of the achievements of the film is to institute a system of visual and material exchange whereby stereotypes themselves appear to become material. Indeed, upon close scrutiny, these stereotypical characters appear almost like marionettes in a theater Lee has created within his film, which can be understood as a *desiring machine*. In fact, as much as stereotypicality in the film is associated with virality and unbridled movement, it is also associated with stiffness and mechanical movement. The larger point is this: if the stereotype is so tangible and suffocating that it acts like a "veneer," then the film's commitment to seeing this materiality through to its most dramatic consequences translates into a commitment to the materiality of the veneer itself. In the film, stereotypicality is increasingly associated with a black coating, whether it is the burnt-cork makeup the entertainers are forced to wear or the audience decides to wear, or the Halloween masks, or the black paint that covers the blackface objects. The argument here is that stereotypes are more things than pictures, or, more precisely, they are pictures *as* things. Thus, the film remains faithful to the etymological meaning of the word "stereotype" as a (fixed) mold used for reproduction.

In this context, whereby the stereotype has too closely adhered to the object, one strategy that might lift the mask from the face, or unstick the coating from the surface beneath it, is to place the stereotype in a dramatic situation, a scene of desire where it might acquire the ability to move and interact with its space and its various dynamics. Once the fetish is unfolded into a scene, as previously discussed, it affords multiple trajectories of identification, or, as Diawara describes it, it enables the performer "to fill all the spaces that the old stereotype occupied and to be the star of the new show."[10]

Greg Tate praises Lee's ability to do so—to make the film align itself with the art that "desires the stereotype" in this way—and describes him as an "expert coonologist," particularly in reference to the sequence of the casting of *Mantan*.[11] "A small ad in *Backstage* had people lining up around the block," Delacroix tells us in a voice-over that introduces a sequence showcasing a parade of diverse and unlikely characters, all seemingly equally desperate to work. The variety of performers also offers Lee the opportunity to underscore diversity in the reactions of Sloan, Delacroix, and another African American network employee who are selecting the show's cast. The first group auditioned is The Roots, who are signed up to play the house band, called the "Alabama Porch Monkeys." Delacroix is obviously taken by their funk. There is a barefoot dancer, stomping around to the beat of an off-screen drum, who elicits some chuckles; a loudly dressed pseudo-comedian singing "I'd be smacking my 'hoes," who causes a collective puzzled reaction; and a bare-chested musician blowing on a long African horn, who gets the most enthusiastic response from the two women: Sloan's standing ovation and her colleague's "post-coital" "thank you." Finally, there is a self-defined Shakespearian actor played by Thomas

Jefferson Byrd—"to be or not to be, that's the motherfucking question," he intones—who eventually lands the part of the show's MC, Honeycutt. He delivers what becomes the refrain of the show: "Niggers *is* a beautiful thing." Struck by the audacious syntactical construction, Delacroix asks Sloan to write it down. Eventually, he emphatically, yet awkwardly, announces, "I am digging that." Overall, the auditions (especially that of the Mau Maus, who walk off the stage, into the audience, and end up standing on the theater seats) begin to introduce the experience of a barely controlled chaos and a sense of a visceral and affective overload, pushing Delacroix to conclude, "I don't want to have anything to do with anything black for at least a week."

Loving and stealing

It is true that the film thematically commits to the question of representation, given that it pivots around a TV writer and other kinds of image-makers or art producers, but it does so to deflect, not endorse, a representational logic by making its referent unavailable. Not only is it impossible to identify the real-life "model" for these representations and objects, but also the film refuses to take a stance about what blackness is, who can define it, and to whom it belongs. Criticized as a dangerous postmodern play with identity, this lack of closure has often been considered the very reason the film's stereotypical images virally proliferate.

One ostensible argument of the film that Delacroix, when speaking to Sloan, uses to explain his decision to write a minstrel show is that media audiences do not want to see blacks "unless they are buffoons"—that there is no real way for black entertainers to appear in public unless they are wearing a more-or-less metaphorical blackface. At the same time, one of the most controversial traits of the film is the uninhibited way in which it shows white America's eager embrace of this old form of entertainment and the extent to which audiences are willing to identify with the "blackness" it makes available. In other words, much controversy is found in the degree to which the film brings this interracial desire to the surface. And, it brings this desire not only to the narrative surface— in the uncensored ways in which it expresses a widespread desire for blackness—but also to the surface of the film image, whereby, as the film progresses, objects, people, and even sets are increasingly coated in black. The film argues that wearing black, or donning black, is a way to "eat" blackness.

Even more profoundly and provocatively, the film handles the dynamic of love and theft as a dominant form of racial relations in popular culture. So, while the proliferation/ accumulation of the iconic blackface image itself accounts for some of the ways the film feels suffocating and affectively overloaded, it does not, in and of itself, fully capture the depth at which love and theft still regulate the entertainment industry and contemporary culture more broadly. In other words, forms of (racist) identification, projection, obsession, and possession might be spectacular, but they are more importantly quotidian and ordinary, and so is their erotic charge.

The character who most embodies this in the film is television executive Dunwitty. He summons Delacroix to his office supposedly to express how he expects him to write a show that will improve the network's ratings but ends up criticizing the extent to which Delacroix is disengaged and alienated from his own blackness: "I am blacker than you . . . I am keeping it real," he asserts. This exchange, therefore, quickly turns into a scene of instruction on the creative energy that Delacroix should derive from his own (disavowed or excessively sanitized) blackness. Dunwitty accuses him of writing shows about white people with black faces. The shows are "too clean . . . too antiseptic." After reading bylines from the shows Delacroix had attempted to pitch in the past, all about middle-class assimilationist characters and situations, Dunwitty concludes that the shows did not get picked up because "nobody—and I mean, no-motherfuckingbody, niggers and crackers alike—want to see that junk." The solution, if there is one, is to be found in the possibility that Delacroix would "dig deep" into his *loins* and find the abject and gritty blackness that will appeal to TV audiences. The reference to Delacroix's loins expresses Dunwitty's injunction to produce "black" content as a process of *secretion* or *extraction*, which reproduces the fantastical relationship between blackness (as black body and identity) and blackface makeup—as if the latter had somehow been extracted from (or secreted by) the former. This image also suggests that both material density/thickness and some form of fluidity are among the requirements for blackness to be successful. This is ultimately the idea behind the very practice of blackening up, that is, the idea that in order to be appealing, blackness has to be somehow turned into a fungible, palpable, and ultimately wearable or ingestible substance.

During this pedagogical moment, the characters are sitting on a corner sofa on one side of Dunwitty's office. Delacroix is tightly enclosed by African statues and flattened against the background. He is framed like an art object, and his mechanical acting, as well as Dunwitty's exaggerated gestures and seemingly unjustified agitation, produce a sense of incongruity of styles and a clash of different material cultures. On one hand, there is high art (or, at least, its pretense), and on the other, pop culture (the sports figures). Not only is there the hovering presence of what I later discuss as mechanical object movement (when Dunwitty repeats the N word, and Delacroix repeats "whitey/whitey/whitey") but also, more broadly, there is the sense that one is watching a stand-up routine taking place in an art gallery.

This scene can easily be read as laying out the conditions for understanding Dunwitty's comments, choices, and bodily movements as stemming from overidentification and infatuation with blackness (the later scene of the pitch makes this plain). But, it also immediately displays an investment in the destabilizing potential of blackface—its self-referentiality as well as the impossibility for it to work as a representation. "I bet you 1,000 dollars you can't tell me who no. 24 is on the wall over there," Dunwitty challenges Delacroix. The writer looks on, perplexed, and cannot answer. Crucially, the camera stays on the two characters and never cuts to the photograph he is supposed to identify. By withholding the reverse shot, the film is already denying an expected representational closure whereby the sign will meet its referent. The purpose of this missed closure goes way beyond the embracing of the mobility of "postmodern identity" or the idea of complete relativity of meaning, as it has been suggested.[12] And its purpose is not just that of playing a trick on the film's audience, who are forced to ponder whether they recognize what turns out to be a photograph of Willie Mays. More profoundly, I believe, this scene begins to establish the film as a strategically malfunctioning philosophical toy. The film is malfunctioning in the sense of attempting to be "present-at-hand" rather than simply "ready-to-hand"; *Bamboozled* is expected to function as a representational machine but refuses to do so. In this way, the film manages to explore the underlying desires that support the very notion of representation—simply put, the desire for race to act as a form of representation of difference.

Later, when Delacroix eventually pitches the idea for the updated minstrel show to Dunwitty, the scene again takes place in his office, but the angle is reversed. Delacroix is sitting on one side of a long conference table, and Dunwitty is sitting underneath the coveted photographs of African American athletes. The scene is distinctive in that it takes on the task of unfolding in space the dynamic of desire and appropriation congealed in the minstrel mask. As Delacroix begins to describe his idea for a minstrel show, Dunwitty becomes increasingly excited. The scene is not shot in the customary shot/reverse-shot structure but rather by alternating increasingly closer and more rapid profile shots of the two men, who, across cut, appear quickly as if in each other's face. As the delivery of the pitch gets more feverish, so does Dunwitty's response. But it is the editing that mostly achieves this effect; this is no longer a dialogue, but instead takes on a "call and response" structure, as the shots get tighter and alternate more rapidly. The long table standing in between them progressively disappears from the frame, and the two men's faces are brought closer and closer to each other. The punch line is the name of the show—*Mantan: The New Millennium Minstrel Show*—and, for this line, the camera is placed on the table directly in front of Delacroix, but at a slightly low angle. He is shown frontally but detached from the space behind him, and the lighting is harsh. As he states the show's name, he fans out his hands to frame his face, thus turning himself into a grotesque mask in a purposeful moment of "self-coonification."

While his hands are still trembling, the camera cuts to a side view and then to a two-shot, showing writer and producer on either side of the table. Dunwitty makes explicit the mounting erotic tension, which the very idea of minstrelsy has already triggered. Pointing at his crotch with his finger, he shares, "You know why I know that I like this? I am getting a boner." Here, the minstrel dynamics of love and theft are dramatized through postures, editing, and camera placement that bring the characters together, almost speaking in each other's face. We see them touching each other *through* the minstrel mask Delacroix's description has conjured. Blackness is something in-between them, both the vehicle and the outcome of their erotic dance.

A minute later, Manray and Womack, the show's two prospective stars, enter the room with Sloan. On the spot, Womack is renamed "Sleep 'N Eat," and both are matter-of-factly told that they'll have to blacken up. After the details of the show have been worked out (that it should be set on a watermelon patch, for example, rather than in the projects— Dunwitty tells Delacroix he wants "none of that gold teeth shit"), Dunwitty demands to get a glimpse of their talent. Unable to contain the energy that comes from the very idea and scenario of a revival of the minstrel show that will recirculate the stock characters of mid-nineteenth-century America, he gets up from the chair, stomps around the room, slaps Delacroix, and yells approvingly, "Delacroix, brother man, you dug deep; deeper than deep." The very process of the resuscitation of these characters seems to reanimate Dunwitty, thus proving Greg Tate's point that blackface expresses a desire to inhabit a more intense (black) way of being human. The innuendo about sexual intercourse/ intimacy continues; with a language that has already shifted to a pre-Emancipation sensibility, Dunwitty demands to "sample the goods." Further, like a bachelor partygoer, he requests a performance that is "raw-dawg and without a bag." As Manray's incredible talent unfolds on top of the table, Dunwitty moves mechanically from side to side, as if attempting to insert himself into the beat of the tap dancing. Here, the shot composition—the camera located at a low angle from behind Dunwitty's head, as he is sitting at one end of the table—implies that Manray is performing a lap dance over Dunwitty's erected phallus.

An allegorical reading of Dunwitty as standing in for the attitude of the entertainment industry as a whole (and as a synecdoche for the viewing public that increasingly gives in to the erotics of black identification) is certainly available and more than justified. The matter-of-fact knowledge that this type of blackness is a hot commodity in the industry is one of the premises of the film. As Dunwitty puts it, "Everybody knows black people set the trends, they set the style." Yet, what type of blackness does the entertainment industry want? To what extent does it have to conform to preexisting assumptions of what blackness is and does—thus effectively repeating the logic, and not just the content, of the stereotype? To what extent does this blackness have to be predictable, known, and recognizable, thereby participating in the dynamic already discussed several times, that of recognition, rather than cognition? In other words, to what extent must blackness act as re-apparition, as *déjà vu*?

The television commercials that precede the television premier of *Mantan: The New Millennium Minstrel Show* make this clear in the way they arguably express an uncensored racial id. One has the sense that what is normally hiding underneath the surface of the language of advertising, in the subtext—and particularly the way in which markers of blackness might be dispersed in a commercial's mise-en-scène for added erotic value—is here, instead, abruptly irrupting into the surface. In this sense, the commercials offer an arrested pass. They pass off as actual commercials, yet not, since they frankly address a series of outrageous fantasies associated with black consumption and black consumers. For example, one scenario deals with the performance of black "johnsons" being further enhanced by a malt liquor—Da Bomb—specially designed by black scientists. Another depicts an environment in which "bitch," as a matter-of-fact way to refer to a woman, is enhanced to the even more disparaging "ho." Finally, a popular fashion designer—satirically named Timmy Hillnigger—speaks earnestly to his consumer base, recommending that they stay broke while continuing to add to his multimillion-dollar corporation. With a self-reflective twist, he further expresses his commitment to his fans: "We keep it so real, we give you the bullet holes." The bullet holes confer a powerful image of a racially repressed content piercing through and tearing the commercial's surface, which, by extension, is also the film's surface. The statement affords a promise of uncensored, unabashed, relentless pouring of content from the racial id, while it reflexively pokes fun at the very expectations wrapped into the idea of "keeping it real."

"Some people just know black people"

The questions of cultural authority and the appropriation of blackness pervade the entire film. They go hand in hand with the fact that, by many accounts, all characters are either stereotypes or caricatures. Yet, they all cling to some idea of cultural authenticity, mixed with various degrees of complacency or militancy. The fluidity of the various trajectories of the appropriation of blackness also prompts the question of who is really "black" in the film. As Dave Chappelle put it in a skit featuring a quiz show where "real" contenders are tested about their knowledge of black popular culture, "Some people just know black people." Provoked by a white person's criticism that his show was offensive to black people, Chappelle decided to put "random" people's knowledge of black people to a test. He assembled a group of archetypical, if not stereotypical, contestants, some of whom are not even addressed by name. They are an African American studies professor from Fordham University, a female New York City police officer stationed in Washington Heights, a writer for *The Chris Rock Show* and *Chappelle's Show*, a Korean grocery store worker, a social worker in Wilmington Delaware, DJ Rob (who claims to have many black friends), a high school student (who claims that most of the boys he goes to school with are black), and a barber from Brooklyn (who claims that 100 percent of his clients are black). During the quiz show, they are asked a variety of questions, such as "What is a Badonkadonk?," "Why do black people love menthol cigarettes so much?," and "Is pimping easy?" In the process of providing their answers, they in turn create fantastical new scenarios—such as when the TV writer, who thinks a "loosey" is a way to describe oral sex rather than a single (i.e., loose) cigarette, rephrases his understanding of a "chickenhead" (which is a way to refer to a whore) as someone who likes "to give a loosey."

A similar situation is laid out in *Bamboozled* during the writers' meeting. Delacroix opens by announcing that he is a straight shooter, telling them that he has had no say in how they have been chosen, and lamenting the fact that there are no other black writers in the room. His throwaway line—"and that Afro does not qualify you, my Jewish friend"—makes reference to the tradition of Jewish entertainers' use of blackface as a primal scene of their own assimilation. Introduced by an extended establishing shot of the room using a slightly low camera angle, Delacroix and Sloan sit at one end of a long and crowded table in front of a giant window. Bathed in light coming through the window, which renders them almost as silhouettes, the scene establishes a collective picture of whiteness. As the meeting begins, racist assumptions are freely traded back and forth across the room—for example, the suggestion that there are no black writers at the meeting because none of them was qualified enough, or didn't want to write for the show, or wouldn't work for the pay, and so on—comments that Delacroix sarcastically rephrases as "maybe they couldn't put down their crack pipes long enough to apply."

After one of the writers rallies the group by insisting on his professionalism and the fact that he is "a damn-good writer and ready to go to work," they all begin to reminisce about their media encounters with blackness, including *Rowan and Martin's Laugh-In*, Pigmeat Markham, *The Jeffersons* and *Good Times!* In so doing, they automatically slide into black impersonation. "Here comes the judge!" exclaims one of the writers, who has deliberately framed his comments with the disclaimer that he is from Iowa, as the film cuts to a brief clip of Markham approaching his bench. Another says, "George and WHEEZY!" as the film cuts to a clip of George Jefferson shouting his wife's name. "Kid DY-NO-MITE!" yells another, as the film cuts to a clip of J. J. Walker saying his catchphrase. The fluidity and ease with which these impersonations occur anticipates the impending wholehearted embrace of blackface by the television audience. At the same time, the film displays its archival commitment, simultaneously suggesting that its internal audience's desire has the ability to initiate these cuts. Thus, the film also displays the melancholic relationship that American audiences nurture toward the place of blackness in media history while the film's editing follows along by showing the clips that *Bamboozled* itself has seemingly incorporated.

When the writers inquire about casting, Delacroix explains that they are going to use black actors in blackface, rather than stars, because blackface would render the stars invisible. To ask an actor like Denzel Washington to put on blackface would be foolish, he explains, and the film again cuts to Denzel Washington as Malcolm X in Spike Lee's earlier film, telling his Harlem audience they have been bamboozled—in other words, that they are complicit with their own manipulation.

Reversing the earlier scene where Dunwitty asks Delacroix to dig into his loins as a black person in order to "extract" the black content audiences really want to see, Delacroix challenges the writers to "tap into [their] white angst" and think about their reaction to the O. J. Simpson trial, the quintessential "melodrama of black and white," as Linda Williams has amply discussed.[13] "How did you feel when the glove did not fit?" he asks, as the film cuts to the corresponding moment from the trial. Then, he urges, "This is your time to purge." Again, the creative process is consistently described as a bodily process of either extraction or secretion, eventually extending to the arousal produced by this "secreted" blackness. After the taping of the pilot, Dunwitty calls Delacroix from his car to let him know that the network executives loved it, and they have ordered twelve episodes, with the show to begin airing in three weeks; he then adds, "They were sweating us."[14]

In a later sequence, the question of cultural authority is approached even more directly. After the airing of the show's premiere, Delacroix and Sloan are called to Dunwitty's office to hear PR consultant Myrna Goldfarb outline the network's response to the controversy the show will predictably spark. She calls it the "*Mantan* Manifesto." This scene occurs right after the second *Mantan* show, when we see Mantan and Sleep 'N Eat enact an updated version of the "indefinite talk" routine from *Stormy Weather* (Andrew Stone, 1943) where dialogue partners chronically cut each other off.[15] Because of that, the routine discusses objects and people who are never named, using pronouns that have no clear referent, and abstractions and hyperboles that create a series of funny non sequiturs. Structurally, even though there is a clear absence at the heart of the exchange, the interlocutors always understand each other. Since there is no clear "it" to the conversation, audiences will fill in the gap. The withholding of closure the film used earlier—when Dunwitty asked Delacroix to identify the baseball player wearing no. 24—now occurs more extensively and systematically in the minstrel routine itself, and it is so conspicuous that it gives the sense of creating an empty space between the sign and its referent. Closer to music than speech, and more affect than content, the rhythm of the indefinite talk determines the pace of the film's editing. When the routine concludes with the entertainers finally exclaiming, "That's perfect!" in unison, it recalls a similar moment earlier in the film when Delacroix and Sloan, who were separately brainstorming about the new show they had been asked to write, both suddenly settle on the same idea, and we see them, in split screen, exclaiming in unison: "Manray!"

In the "*Mantan* Manifesto" sequence, Ms. Goldfarb and Delacroix continue a similar pattern of non sequiturs. They are sitting across one another around the conference table, with Dunwitty in the middle. Ms. Goldfarb and Delacroix's exchange underscores the continuity between what happens on the recreated minstrel stage and what happens in the "outside world." It thus highlights the portability of the possibility of (moral and aesthetic) license set up by the former space. Many of Dunwitty's comments are insulting. "*Mantan* Manifesto!" she announces proudly, and continues, "Catchy, ain't it?" "So is syphilis," he drily replies. She boasts, "I got my PhD in African-American studies from Yale." "So, you fucked a Negro in college" is Delacroix's retort, which Dunwitty interrupts by asking him to keep the conversation "above the belt." Delacroix's comebacks are timely and his satire biting, and this dialogue creates a comical call-and-response, with each response offering an inverted mirror image of the structure of the previous sequence. For example: "The best defense is offense," states Ms. Goldfarb. "I thought it was the other way around," answers Delacroix. "Exactly, I think we are on the same page," she immediately concludes.

To diffuse the connection between Mantan, Sleep 'N Eat, and race, and deflect the accusation of leveraging stereotypical character traits, Goldfarb proposes to present them as two "slackers" instead: "I took a couple of years off after graduate school and walked the European countryside—it's not that big of a deal," she offers. This is a failed counterfactual. The equal exchange imagined by this comparison fails to carry out its promise of equality, which had already been undermined by the plethora of non sequiturs leading up to it, that is, instances of failed or inconclusive exchange. At the same time, it gestures toward another possibility—that it is blackness that fills the space between the non sequiturs. Both during the minstrel show routine and in this exchange, there is an "it" that is being constructed, something that only functions successfully in the former—where it achieves an effect of seamlessness, while also highlighting the performers' artistry—yet fails during the exchange with Ms. Goldfarb. Retrospectively, one realizes how emphatic the film is about the "mechanics" of comedy—timing, pacing, actors' chemistry, and body language—and how complicit the editing is in creating a successful comedic effect.

In one last attempt to enlist Delacroix's support for her proposed "*Mantan* Manifesto," Ms. Goldfarb asserts that "the network's best asset is you," to which a surprised Delacroix replies, "Me?" This exchange—possibly the only one in which the two are "in sync"—is repeated twice. The fact that it is not immediately clear whether the characters repeated their lines or not makes human speech and movement appear unnatural and mechanical, while the editing seems to stutter. More importantly, the film presents Delacroix as more of an automaton than a living person because of the repeated mechanical movement of his arm, which prefigures the (eventually self-moving) jolly nigger bank.

Who's blak?

Ms. Goldfarb's clumsy endorsement of Delacroix is entirely instrumental to a simplistic racial essentialism: the "show can't be racist because you are black." Yet, even this desperate appeal to cultural authority ultimately fails. As Sloan promptly corrects her, "That's where you are wrong. See, he is not black—he's a Negro." This exchange calls attention to one of the overall effects of the mobilization of the conceit of blackface in the film—that is, to pose the question of who and what is ultimately black (as already indicated, the film peremptorily refuses to answer this). Both the struggle for cultural authority and the multiple trajectories of appropriation of blackness in the film destabilize the notion of authenticity and show the fundamental variability and expansiveness of blackness. Again, *Bamboozled* continues to call attention to how blackness is often the product of an interaction or exchange, as we see in the sequence of Delacroix's pitch.

To be sure, the film is not confused about who is black and who isn't (which is one of the reasons Dunwitty is so outrageously funny and yet pathetic at the same time) but it is also aware that "blackness"—as an imaginary, a repertoire of gestures, a mode of expression, a cultural reference—is constantly made and remade. Of course, blackness is not only made by black people. The cultural repertoire that is produced by black impersonators, whether they are in blackface or not, might fully become part of black popular culture (just like "giving a loosey" may one day be incorporated in black slang, as Chappelle concluded at the end of the skit). In other words, with equal determination, the film poses the question of who the "real" black people are just as much as it constructs blackness as an increasingly tangible *thing*, which is built through tremendous cooperation between different parties. Sometimes, as I show later, blackness attaches to whatever gets "tossed around,"—an object, a line, an idea—as happens in several scenes involving the Mau Maus.

The only ostensibly direct answer to the question "Who/what is black?" is, in fact, offered by the rappers. Their answer is quite highbrow—an act of "signifyin(g)" in the sense of creating a *difference* in the signifier "black"—even though the way they arrive at this answer is not.[16] The scene takes place immediately after the sequence of the pitch for the TV show. The next cut takes us to a dark, smoke-filled room where the

Mau Maus are huddled together around a mixing console, conspicuously drinking Da Bomb and Hennessy liquor. Wearing a black T-shirt with the inscription, "The African Hellaucaust," and, below that, a stylized reproduction of the iconic image of the slave ship Brookes, Big Blak Afrika immediately bursts out: "The name of this shit right here . . . Black is black . . . The name of the album is 'The Black Album.'" The camera tilts to the left, as if mounted onto a rocking boat, before cutting to close-ups of various band members. Smooth Blak (played by Charli Baltimore), who is sucking from a lollipop, makes the case for spelling "black" without the "c"—B-L-A-K—as an act of nonconformity with the white man's world. There are several apparently random cuts—including, in the middle of sentences, a profile shot of a huge Afro being combed with an Afro-pick—and small swinging camera movements, which convey a sense of floating around the room in a quasi-circular fashion.

Shown from an extremely low angle, 1/16th begins to rap on a series of negative connotations associated with the word "black." After spitting a long list, including "black . . . angry . . . sullen . . . depressed," all punctuated by the group's "yeahs," he concludes, "must have been a white guy who started all that!" as the band cheers in unison. The pace of the editing confirms to the beat of the rapping, thus displaying an incipient machine-like editing pattern, which is important for the way the film incorporates the viewers' desire into its own movement. Part of the satirical bent of the sequence lies in its tautology: black is black, and, even though it becomes "Blak" through a signifyin(g) gesture, there is really no clear content or referent to it, a fact that matches the lack of clarity the rap group has about its own political and artistic commitments and motivations. Rendered through repetition, iteration, and accumulation, blackness here is nothing but performance. It is a performance, however, that accrues a certain amount of density by virtue of repetition: if you say "black" over and over again, or if you "build" blackness by tossing it around, it might become something to which you can hold on.

These dynamics of appropriation, expropriation, and impersonation of blackness ultimately converge in the performance of blackness demanded by the minstrel show. Different from the "primal scene" of blackface in the Hollywood musical, which offers a spectacle of assimilation, in *Bamboozled*, blackening up in front of the mirror crystalizes instead a realization of self-alienation for black entertainers who have to collude with their own process of fetishization. In this sense, the blackening up scene is the epitome of the inverted mirror stage, insofar as it introduces a situation where the self is both split and doubled into an object and an Other.[17] In this "mirror of abjection," the black entertainer experiences the blackness he is about to perform as both part of, and other than, himself.[18]

Bamboozled contains three of these mirror scenes. In each, the mirror functions consistently as a figure for the relationship between image, self, and objecthood. In Lee's variation of this scene, however, the mirror is not simply a conduit to self-alienation but also an outlet to self-reification or self-mattering. Blacking up ushers in a transition toward thingness that complements the materiality of the blackness the entertainer is forced to apply.

The first scene, which occurs before the taping of the show's pilot, is introduced by Sloan's voiceover narration and describes the results of her research on blackening up and the various material components and gestures required to perform this ritual. She begins by making the programmatic statement that "we should . . . keep the ritual the same." Her voice-over accompanies several extreme close-ups of the process of burning the cork down to a crisp, adding alcohol, firing it up, adding water, and mixing it into a black paste. Then, the entertainers are shown applying it to their faces in medium shot, from behind their backs, in order to show their double reflection in the mirror. There are profile shots of Womack angrily looking into the mirror while he is applying the burnt cork paste to his face and close-ups of Manray, seemingly less perturbed. Eventually, the camera shows only their mirror reflection within a split-screen effect. When Sloan's voice-over intones, "Final detail is the lips. The redder the lips, the better. So I suggest fire truck red," we see extreme close-ups of the performers' lips. The sequence ends with the word "showtime" distributed between the two performers: Womack says "show," while we see a split mirror image with his back in it, and, after a quick cut, Manray says "time," in profile, while his white gloves frame his face.

Throughout the sequence, the camera angles privilege multiple mirror reflections, thus offering a correlative of the psychic splitting of this inverted mirror phase. Reading this scene through a deliberate combination of the Lacanian mirror and the Freudian "uncanny" as conveying the idea of the difficulty to distinguish between "me" and "not me"— the idea of a double that is split off from the self—Gregory Laski emphasizes that this scene shows how "the retroactive image of the body in pieces comes about in response to the anticipatory image of the ideal self."[19] Furthermore, the subject is not simply alienated by his identification with an ideal image but, instead, shattered by his dispersal in a number of "black" things: the pitch-black paste, the fire truck-red lips, etc. Sloan's striking recommendation to "please put on cocoa butter to protect your skin," brings the performer face-to-face with the brute matter that the minstrel show equates with his blackness; not only is the performer forced to seek himself mirrored in things, but must also find himself in an undifferentiated black "stuff." In this sense, Sloan's recommendation crystalizes just how extraneous this "stuff" is to the black body that has supposedly "secreted" it. For a moment during this sequence, we see some of David Levinthal's framed photographs of black collectibles hanging on the dressing room wall and reflected in the mirror; they function like the computer-generated images (CGIs) of puppets introducing the TV premiere, insofar as they display the anticipation of the marketing of their minstrel image as an object, while also keeping the "me" and "not me" in the same frame.

The second mirror scene follows Delacroix's reflection on his visit to Junebug. "My father was a broken man . . . he had principles," he comments in voice-over, while driving back from the comedy show, expressing his resolve that "it was not going to happen to me." There is a sudden cut to the cork burning and the black paste being made—vivid reminders of conditions to which he would not agree, but has nevertheless engineered for other performers. This second mirror scene has faster cuts and more extreme camera angles; more time is spent on the entertainers' faces, and Womack appears nervous and angry, while Manray seems perplexed. Eventually, the camera shows Womack's split mirror image framed by his white gloves; this time, he says "showtime" by himself, and, as the camera pulls back, tears are visible in his eyes.

Finally, during the third scene, the shots are even closer to the performers' faces, and the transitions between them are mostly dissolves, thus underscoring that a blurring of boundaries between the performer and the character, the face and the mask, has already occurred. At the scene's conclusion, Manray's double reflected image appears in the background of the same frame as Womack's profile. Womack whispers "Sleep 'N Eat" while his hand "caresses" the double reflected image of Manray's face.

The location of the camera, the refusal to cut between shots, and this final impossible image (given that the two performers sit side by side in the dressing room) dramatically render a system of exchanges and assemblages between people and things. The film has been building toward this system with moments that establish a visual equivalence between Delacroix and recognizably black objects—for instance, the African sculptures in Dunwitty's office. In other words, if the blackface is the mask (the fetish *and* the stereotype, as previously suggested), Lee herein counters its logic of closure and fixation by *unfolding it* in space and placing it within dramatic situations. Aesthetically and formally, the film interprets the mirror scene capaciously, not simply as a moment of reflection, but also as a scene of exchange.

Dancing with mirrors, dancing with things

After the successful premiere of the show, Sloan gifts Delacroix an authentic cast-iron "Jolly Nigger" bank, circa turn of the century, and invites him to interact with it. Sloan is the historian, the archivist, and, in many ways, the historical consciousness of the film. In giving this object to Delacroix, she is already making a connection between the stereotypes he has revived and these black collectibles that remind her of a time "when black people were considered inferior, subhuman . . . we should never forget." In doing this, she is also asking that we think of stereotypes as *mechanical things* animated by our desire. Sloan first demonstrates how the object works—you put a coin in the toy's hand, then press a lever, and it will bring it to its mouth, where it disappears—and then encourages Delacroix to "give it a whirl" (his words), which he does. While "dancing" with the thing, Delacroix enters into an assemblage with the object and, in the process, acquiesces to the fact that, as commodity form (i.e., the *form* of commodity status) their common blackness is the strongest conduit for this assemblage to take place. They "assemble" because they are both "black."

The interaction with the Jolly Nigger bank can also be regarded as a mirror scene, as can all other interactions Delacroix has with the other collectibles that accumulate in his office. Sloan's gift, in fact, has unleashed a hoarding instinct in Delacroix, who begins to collect more and more objects. After getting off the phone with his mother, who unceremoniously tells him that she is disappointed in him, he turns to the statuette of a slave child with moving eyes and a head that swings like a metronome. The child-object is standing on the coffee table, beside his sofa, and is framed at equal height: "What the hell are you smiling at?" he asks. Prompted by the mise-en-scène and the framing, which have already established an effect of equivalence between them, he too interpellates the object as an interlocutor, as equal. Throughout the phone call, the object appears comparatively livelier than him, since it continues to move back and forth, while Delacroix reacts motionlessly to the highly dramatic assessment his mother makes of the show he wrote.

Bamboozled also contains moments of disavowal of the imposed mirror image. The first happens when Delacroix shows Manray and Womack a tape of the original Mantan Moreland acting in *The Gray Ghost*. "He was a clown; a bit of a buffoon; very funny," Delacroix says. "This ain't funny," Womack immediately retorts. Shortly after, Manray presses on, "How does he make his eyes do that?" he asks, while watching a close-up of Moreland seemingly enlarging his eyes and shaking mechanically as he is about to roll some dice. "He was gifted," replies Delacroix without hesitation. Here again, a mirror scene also becomes a moment of interrogation of the object, since Mantan Moreland presents an object movement that Manray cannot recognize. For Kara Keeling, this moment in the film expresses the crisis, brought by the regime of the digital image, of the connection between the filmic image and a profilmic reality that it is supposed to unproblematically reflect.[20] *Bamboozled* puts the image at a remove from "the Black" and, therefore, exposes a crisis of representation that was always already there: blacks never matched their media representations. In other words, the tension that the filmic image, whether photochemical or digital, cannot resolve is precisely that between recognizing it as "me" or "not-me." At moments like this, the film acknowledges that "photographic" representation never served the black subject. Even more profoundly, it might signal the beginning of a dissatisfaction with the idea of the media image as mirror of the subject and move closer to "unburdening representation," that is, seeking relief from the desperate attempt to establish "an authentic relation to an inauthentic and oppressive world."[21]

After explaining the idea behind the satirical minstrel show to Womack and Manray, Delacroix explicitly evokes one of the few recognized historical exceptions to this fact, which is the deployment of photography in support of the tactics of the

Civil Rights movement. To bolster his idea that the show can be socially relevant, Delacroix explains to Sloan, "The Reverend Martin Luther King did not enjoy seeing his people beaten on the evening news." He is therefore appealing to a specific relationship of trust that news photography had established with its public at that time; this trust was a result of the direct involvement of mostly northern photographers, who placed themselves in the "thick" of the action in order to capture the images that eventually catalyzed support for the Civil Rights cause (Charles Moore's photographs of the fire hoses and the Birmingham dogs are a prominent example). Photography and the news media were so important that Martin Luther King engineered the Birmingham campaign (among others) in such a way that it would guarantee media coverage. While Delacroix is talking, the clip from *The Gray Ghost* continues to roll in the background, showing Mantan Moreland getting his face splashed with water. Rather than an example of what Delacroix is arguing, we see yet another instance of object movement within the mediatic frame, but this also suggests that this imagery has the power to outlive even the trustworthy and politically relevant documentary imagery produced during the Civil Rights movement.

Later, while watching the TV premiere of *The New Millennium Minstrel Show*, Manray is deliberately and justifiably "waiting for himself," but, at this point, his expectation can better be described as a *delusion of representation* because of his attachment to wanting to approach the CGI dancing puppets that precede the broadcast as a *portrayal* of himself and Womack. Rather than disavowing what he sees on screen as "not me," he asks, "Why did they make my nose so big?" Sloan simply replies, "You have every right to be upset." Once it is rendered as a scene of exchange with the object, the "mirror" scene becomes a way in which the racial assemblage is formed. So, as much as the subject might want to disavow this equivalence with the object, the two are already conjoined.

This dancing with things is also a way to get in touch with (and touch) the past. Here is where the archival and hauntological commitment of the film come together. As Delacroix amasses collectibles, he is almost swallowed up by them, and he is eventually ushered through to "the other side," that is, the "hole" behind the mask where he comes into contact with a bottomless past he didn't know could be so powerful. And, as the studio audience increasingly dons blackness, it, too, threatens to absorb the performers. In turn, Manray and Womack develop the fear that they have become what they thought they were only performing.

Dances with things in *Bamboozled* ultimately become scenes of instruction that occur, for example, in the interactions with objects such abecedaries and piggy banks, like those discussed by Robin Bernstein and Bill Brown. Burnt-cork makeup must also be regarded as such an object, as it creates a racial assemblage around *coerced* movement. In fact, "performing," in the context of minstrelsy, does not have the connotation of flexibility, creativity, and self-invention that it has when we usually talk about the performativity of race, which is a way to insist on the lived possibility of departing from already predetermined scripts. In other words, it brings up a question of volition vs. the "automatic" (and automaton-like) nature of the minstrel performance, which, even in its brilliance, involves a considerable amount of scripted stiffness in order to conform to very rigid protocols of the genre. Besides, even though Womack and Manray have freely entered the contract that binds them to the show, they are now held captive by its demands to collude with the minstrel mask.

Animation and reanimation

The subject/object relation, the assemblage with the object, the scene of exchange, and dances with the objects themselves are all relations that have direct bearing on the political ontology of blackness, that is, on how and in what circumstances the black subject is fully part of the human fold. The question of self-motivated movement, for example, is crucial to the ontological distinction between subject and object, the human and the nonhuman, the living and the nonliving, because motility is traditionally interpreted as a sign of agency. "Motility" in this case refers to a movement that is performed by one's volition rather than that prompted, initiated, or demanded by another's desire. It is the opposite of not only coercion but also of automatism. Thus, the very heart of the film, from the point of view of its stance on this ontological question, is the scene of the "revenge of the memorabilia," where the object Delacroix had danced with—the Jolly Nigger bank—in turn, begins to dance of its own will and therefore exacts a revenge on its Frankenstein-like collector.

This crucial scene follows Delacroix's phone call with his mother. The movement of the statuette he addressed shortly before had visually prefigured the sound of a metronome, a sound that now fills the room. Delacroix sits at his desk and begins to play with the Jolly Nigger bank. He puts one coin after the other on its hand and, with each clicking sound of the cast-iron arm lifting up to the toy's mouth, the film cuts to a canted still shot showing one of the collectibles perched on Delacroix's bookcase. Suddenly, the cuts accelerate, and the shots are at closer range, with even more drastically canted angles, emphasizing the object's facial features in a way that reproduces the aesthetics of Levinthal's blackface photographs.[22]

The scene is framed as hypothetical through Delacroix's voice-over: "When I thought, or imagined, that my favorite Jolly Nigger bank, an inanimate object, a piece of cold cast iron, was moving by itself, I knew I was getting paranoid. Did I really see what I saw, or was I hallucinating?" From the point of view of the film, this is irrelevant, since the movement has already occurred, and Delacroix now exists in this (hypothetical? counterfactual?) world of animate objects. The sense of "animation" comes partly from the piggy bank's arm actually raising repeatedly to its mouth and partly from the way its sound, as well as the sound of the metronome before, brings a sense of movement to the still, canted shots of the other collectibles. Shot with emphasis on their eyes while they are sitting silent and still in the depth of the visual field, these artifacts suddenly become beholders of a gaze that interrogates Delacroix and questions his choices. They claim their liveliness, their sentience, their volition.

By staging the self-motivated and self-propelled movement of the object, the film also stages the reenactment of the systemic breakdown of the distinction between humans and things and "the recollection of the ontological scandal perpetrated by slavery" in the form of a reanimation of the black body reified in these objects.[23] Delacroix's demise coincides precisely with this discovery of the fundamental continuum between himself and the black collectibles that vengefully come back to life. Bill Brown notably described the "American uncanny" as this return, through the form of animation of a mechanical object, of the personhood that had been wiped from the slave. Referring back to the essay by Ernst Jenstch that inspired Freud's own writing on the uncanny, Brown emphasizes how the uncanny emerges from the impossibility to distinguish the animate from the inanimate and the living from the dead. For him, the "unfamiliar" suddenly appearing in the familiar—or, the "return of the repressed" in American culture—is the collapsed ontological distinction between persons and things. The ontological instability expressed by the Jolly Nigger bank represents what he calls the "material unconscious" of the film.

We can further understand the American uncanny along the axis of processes of reification, thus focusing on how the person of the slave is turned into a thing and how such thingness authorizes the mass production of household objects toward which similar social relations can continue to be expressed—a second-degree reification, since it further reifies the thingness of the slave by solidifying the black body into a tangible object. The American uncanny can also be seen through the idea of trauma, in the sense of understanding the revival of the minstrel show as the repetition of a traumatic event that cannot be accessed as part of the past because it was never assimilated to it. Thus, it is constantly reenacted in the present without a sense of a clear distinction between remembering and repeating. In this sense, the American uncanny further refers to the strange familiarity of the minstrel imagery, which creates the hauntological effect of a re-apparition.

In formal terms, we can finally understand the uncanny as emphasizing continuity between poles that are normally opposed: animate/inanimate, living/not living, remembrance/repetition, me/not me, then/now, and so on. Aesthetically, this is achieved in the film by charging black surfaces with the task of initiating a scene of exchange between these poles. In other words, a certain amount of visual likeness becomes key to the system of equivalences the film creates between subject and object. Blackness is where things and persons trade places; the blackness of the racist collectibles emphasizes their exchangeability with blackface makeup, and the universal application of burnt cork on the faces of the entertainers and the studio audience emphasizes their exchangeability and uniformity as a new type of "people" constituted by the minstrel spectacle itself.

Not only are many faces metaphorically or literally black in the film, but blackness is also a vehicle of "facialization." To gain a "face," a recognizable site of personhood, Brown observes, even the racist collectibles have to "blacken up." By doing so, they suggest that blackface might be the uncanny face of American commodity culture. Or, said differently, blackness is the American commodity form *par excellance*, that is, the way in which commodity status becomes visible in American culture. Or, in still other terms, since the slave was a commodity, commodity fetishism is always haunted by the confusion between person and thing. This is the reason scenes of exchange in *Bamboozled* are so important, because they operate hauntologically: from a hauntological perspective, the very fact of exchange, that is, the *equation* between objects and things, retroactively conjures up the specter of equality.

Thinking about the commodity form as "black" emphasizes the process whereby blackness brings commodity status to the surface. This is obvious when we think about the use of the black surface just described, that is, the man-made coating of faces and things, but it is a bit less so when the commodity form is dispersed in the mise-en-scène or across the surface of the image. In other words, black objects are not the only manifestation of the commodity form in the film. The commercials that introduce *Mantan*'s premiere, in particular, show how disseminated the commodity form can be in the digital era.

To appreciate this complicated sequence, which I have already discussed from an entirely different angle, two things are needed. First, the awareness that digital filmmaking is one of the provocative choices that Lee made in shooting *Bamboozled*. It was a financial necessity he was able to turn into a remarkably productive aesthetic principle because it afforded very quick filmmaking, with a number of cameras rolling at the same time, thus allowing for a compelling proliferation of points of view. Second, and consequently, within the logic of filmmaking that was being negotiated at the turn of the millennium—when celluloid still stood as a sign of "love for the object" against digital video's cheapness, disposability, and aesthetic inadequacy—the decision to shoot the sequences of the minstrel show in Super 16 mm indicate a commitment to fully render the vibrancy of the colors, sets, costumes, and objects in the minstrel show. Thus, the sequence of the commercials stages a (meta) mise-en-scène of exchange between the photochemical and the digital with expressive means that are specific to each: the photochemical stands on the side of the integrity of the object by emphasizing its sensuous properties, while the digital image stands on the side of movement, dispersion, and dissemination.

Here is how it happens. The sequence begins with a CGI animated title sequence showing a theatrical backdrop featuring a huge minstrel mouth that opens to let out two dancing hard-plastic puppets modeled after the show's two stars. With oversized heads and lips over a pitch black body, the puppets look like bobbleheads, thus foreshadowing the show's ability to generate a plethora of consumer objects to satisfy its desiring audience. The tactile digital aesthetics (a la *Toy Story*, where the slick CGI creates a skin for the film that feels as cool and smooth as a Fisher-Price toy) model the audience's reaction to the show—the desire to touch and own.[24] The television audience at home encounters the entertainers first as "toys"—that is, disposable, available, and functional to one's enjoyment—before it ever sees them in the (blackface-coated) "flesh." Here, as already mentioned, there is a striking moment of misrecognition—Manray exclaims, "Why did they make my lips so big?" Yet, why such an instinctive "identification" with the object? What might ultimately enable this delusion of representation?

Because of its tactility and the vibrancy of its colors, the image of the CGI puppets appears closer to the analog image of the minstrel show than to the "degraded" pixelated image of the commercials that immediately follow. It is a transitional image that ushers in another transition the sequence wants to convey—a shift between two stages of the commodity form of blackness: blackness as attached to an identifiable commodity object (the puppets, and before that, the collectibles) and blackness as a dispersed and diffused commodity aesthetics visualized in the commercials. Both "Da Bomb" and the Timmy Hillnigger clothing line are targeted to black urban youth, and it is precisely this idea of blackness as their desirable destination that bestows an erotic patina to the advertised product. In other words, blackness here is not the property of an object but rather a language and a sensibility. In this way, the commercials participate in the larger advertising aesthetics of "capitalist realism" and therefore partake of the same self-referential logic. The commercials employ the idiom of a caricatured hip-hop aesthetics, and trust the excessively moving bodies—bumping, rubbing, twerking—with the task of producing a distributed sense of "blackness" as the interface that enables capitalist realism to say "I love you" to itself.

Similarly, in the scene of the live feed of Manray's execution, all TV viewers are shot in a stark silver light, and their skins are almost equally silver-gray. The court injunction to have the

Internet footage of the "Dance of Death" carried by television networks gestures toward the idea of a universal media public, a possibility that was still very much in question at the turn of the millennium, when the technological divide across racial lines was still very pronounced. In the film, this divide is judicially overcome in order to bring the people what they want. Thus, the forced broadcast functions as an extension of the same dynamic already occurring in the minstrel show, wherein the audience constitutes itself as a "people" when their differences are sublimated by the very spectacle of the reconciled otherness (i.e., the melancholic body of black impersonation) they are viewing. In the scenes of the taping of the minstrel show, the studio audience's donning of blackface makes "the people" emphatically visible because they are unified under one common signifier. But, in this scene, the film's cinematography pushes its most recognizably "digital" elements to the fore in order to create a sense of visual uniformity; now it is a grayish light, not blackface makeup, that homogenizes the audience's faces.

Animating audiences

The mise-an-abyme structure of the film produces multiple internal audiences so that the film can explore how they are constructed and activated. As Alice Maurice argues, Lee conceived of the live studio audience of the minstrel show to both model and mirror the diegetic television audience and the extra-diegetic theater audience for the film itself. He therefore created situations in which he could both engineer and examine how all of these audiences are progressively animated.

The studio audience's response to *Mantan* is built slowly and carefully, in such a way that looking at the show and looking at one another's reactions to it are crucial to the audience's ultimate unification under the blackface makeup. Lee has said that, for the show's pilot, many of the audience members did not know that Glover and Davidson were going to wear blackface, so he had several cameras record the audience's "live" immediate reactions. Visibly uncomfortable, the white audience members, in particular, look nervously around to African American audience members to determine whether it is alright to clap along. Audience participation increases with each taping of *Mantan*, and by the last show, when Manray refuses to blacken up and appears on stage in his street clothes, all audience members—including Dunwitty, who is watching from the control room—are wearing blackface, while Honeycutt openly questions them about whether or not they identify as "niggers." Strategically, Lee gave the group of extras who compose the studio audience a "blacking up" kit to prepare for the shoot, so that they would undergo the same process that the show's two stars and countless other black and white entertainers had to (or chose to) undergo.

Maurice regards the accumulating black figurines in Delacroix's office as one of the film's internal audiences, which increases in number as *Mantan's* television audience increases in size. The first member among them is the Jolly Nigger bank, but its mechanical movement had already been anticipated by the film's editing in the scene of the *Mantan Manifesto*, when Delacroix's reaction to Ms. Goldfarb's assertion that he is the biggest asset of the show provokes Delacroix's shocked reaction: "Me?" "Yes you," she replies. The bank is a frozen version of Delacroix's already mechanical existence, to be sure, but it is also its witness.

All of the film's internal audiences become progressively animated in a variety of ways—not only by the melancholic spectacle itself, but also through "mechanical" means (specific studio instructions to applaud, howl, etc.) and through the actual humor of the minstrel routines, which eventually solicits the laughter of some of *Mantan's* most critical viewers: Sloan, Delacroix, and even one of the Mau Maus. Maurice describes *Mantan* as a "laughjerker" (evoking Linda Williams's description of melodrama as a tearjerker in her famous essay on body genres), an effect produced by the extension of the reach of automatism to all the diegetic concentric audiences and to the film's audience as well. In other words, Lee strives to produce the effect of "canned laughter," which also features in Elia Kazan's *A Face in the Crowd* (1957), a film that, together with Sidney Lumet's *Network* (1976), was a crucial inspiration for *Bamboozled*.[25] Ultimately, this structure, composed of several internal audiences, is responsible for constructing the entire film as a "desiring machine" moved by the audiences themselves. One way this desire is mobilized is through the creation of various effects of "liveness."

The minstrel show already stands as a (comparatively) "live" version of the stereotypical characters represented in the racist collectibles and functions as their animated, fleshed-out, fully embodied form. It does so not only because, as a genre, it is the apotheosis of pantomime, but also because of its insistence on multiple effects of liveness. Shot in Super 16, *Mantan* stands out as more vibrant than the rest of the film due to its saturated colors, lavish mise-en-scène, and the sheer energy that comes from the actors' movements. Further, the funk of the Alabama Porch Monkeys includes frequent shifts in pace and rhythm, accentuating the free-flowing lines of dialogue and the vibrant choreography. Liveness also emerges from the very fact that the show's popularity underscores the vitality of these archetypal stereotypical figures. Another effect of liveness emerges from these sequences' emphasis on embodiment, which is marked by the vivid sounds of bodies moving on stage (the thumps and taps of the performers), the actors' exaggerated and incredibly fluid gesturing, and the visual evidence of the labor of performing (sweat, spit, and so on). Ultimately, the revival of some of the minstrel show's original humor makes contemporary viewers recognize black entertainers' intelligence at work behind the required buffoonery and reveals the edgy brand of comedy that was being shared through minstrelsy, along with the rich cultural heritage that fueled these performances. (This is an echo of what Lott says about minstrelsy's recognition of an existing black culture.)

At the same time, the juxtaposition of Delacroix's private audience (i.e., the collectibles) with the studio audience suggests a strange continuity between the reanimated inanimate object and the "live" recorded performance. Thus, it calls attention to the point that, due to the very fact that it is prerecorded, the "live" studio audience is already more dead than alive; to put it differently, television's ideology of liveness might already be a form of resuscitation. The image of group identity that the studio audience in the film ultimately produces is mob-like and rather frightening. And, even though Manray's execution is carried out by the Mau Maus, the film presents minstrelsy as "the repressed element in the mixture of authenticity and automatism that constructs the mass audience."[26]

"I 'spect I grow'd"

The effects of liveness and self-initiated movement are also characteristics of commodity fetishism. Again, the compulsively moving slave, Topsy, offers a prototype for this convergence of self-origination and liveness. This is the *"I 'spect I grow'd. Don't think nobody never made me"* effect, that is, a vitality that depends on the way the commodity effaces the labor that produced it. Similarly, *Bamboozled* effaces the work that viewers' desire performs to animate the minstrel figures. In the minstrel skit about parents and, or *as,* mates, however, this labor returns as a focus on the conjunction of production and reproduction in plantation economy. The skit is worth addressing in its entirety. Womack opens his routine with, "I don't know who I is," to which Mantan replies, "Well, I'll be an Alabama Porch Monkey's Uncle," followed by a cut to a band member combing his Afro with an afro pick and Womack's relieved reaction, "Least you know who you is!" He then continues, "Years ago I married a widow who had a grown-up daughter. My daddy visit us often, fell in love and married her. Thusly, he became my son-in-law, and my step-daughter became my mother because she was my father's wife. That's right ... After that my father's wife gave birth to a son. Which became my brother ... AND my grandchild because he was the son of my daughter." Mantan rejoins, "What!? You jivin'!" and Womack continues, "I ain't jivin'! Now, accordingly, my wife was my grandmother because she was my mother's mother. Mantan, I was my wife's husband and grandchild at one and the same time. And, lo and behold, as the husband of a person's grandmother is a grandfather [. . .] I became my goddamned own grandfather!"

The skit concludes with Mantan's bewildered reaction, "OHHH, Holy Mackerel! Sleep-n-Eat that SHOOOO is a whopper!" Womack's blessing follows: "You said it Cousin!" Then comes their simultaneous question, "Or is We?"

Here, rather than a missing link between statements or the construction of an undisclosed object (as in the "indefinite talk" routine), the theme is incest as a mode of production. Suddenly, Womack bursts into a dance adapted from his own (i.e., Tommy Davidson's) stand-up routine, set to the tune of "You Ain't Never Seen No Nigger Sitting Here with a Fiddle." Just like Topsy, Womack's liveliness is such that he has metaphorically *leaped* out of the page. The effect of this impromptu transition proves irresistible even to one of the Mau Maus watching the show, who bursts into laughter, despite the condemning looks of the other members. "This shit is funny to me" is his excuse.

Eyes everywhere

Lee has been criticized for displaying an ambivalent attitude toward the racist collectibles that accumulate on the film's sets, and his camerawork has even been described as "lingering" and "caressing" the objects. The curiosity the film expresses toward its artifacts is undeniable; both the minstrel show and the racist collectibles are stunning visual/material culture artifacts, and they *demand* to be addressed. In particular, Lee's way of framing the collectibles is directly indebted to both

Levinthal's monumentalization of those same objects and his commitment to leveraging their aesthetic and sensual qualities for the purpose of reanimating them. "You have to wonder what type of mind it takes to turn that hatred into a wind-up toy," Lee asked.[27] This process of reanimation is not a way to glorify but rather to squarely pose the ontological question to which the film is committed. In other words, how do these processes of reification get initiated?

On a different level, this ambivalence highlights the commitment to critically leveraging the commodity fetish as the animated version of an object—its radiant, lively, "Topsy" version—including the possibility that it might harbor a point of view into the system of which it is part. In the film, this is rendered by the way the editing strings together the inputs coming from various consumer-grade digital cameras employed in each scene, thus creating the sensation of a proliferation of points of view, along with the feeling that the film is being assembled as we are watching it. Manray and Womack, in particular, are associated with the distributed gaze of the commodity fetish, at least until their movements are subsumed within, and formalized by, the automaton-like movements of the minstrel stage.

The scene where they attempt to enter the CNS building to force a meeting with Delacroix capitalizes on the possibility of having several cameras running at all times. It begins with their attempt to enter through the revolving door, which is seen from a camera already inside the building. As they get inside, the scene cuts to a series of extreme close-ups of their interaction with the security guards, including from across the 180° line and from a surveillance camera mounted on the security desk. These chaotic cuts match Womack and Manray's attempts to ask for Delacroix, even though they cannot recall his name. There is a quasi-slapstick moment as they roll out a variety of last names that begin with "Dela"—Delapointe, Delapot, Delasomething—to which one of the security guards sarcastically answers, "And De La Soul is not here, either." The fast-paced and hectic cutting just described does not "stabilize" until the elevator doors open, with Sloan suddenly appearing and delivering a perfectly intelligible sentence: "These are associates of Mr. *Delacroix*." She pushes them into the elevator and takes them to see him.

Pushing this conceit even further, in the scene of the live feed of the "Dance of Death," the image broadcast on the diegetic TV screen originates within the diegetic field. Manray is tied to a chair sitting on top of a wooden platform, which is very similar to the makeshift stage he was carrying along at the beginning of the film, and there is a TV set on his left showing the live feed that the networks picked up as result of the court injunction. The character 1/16th Blak, who is present in the scene, shoots the images we see on the TV screen. The mise-en-abyme structure of the film collapses here into a loop: live action, broadcast image (i.e., the image of the execution shot by 1/16th), and its source all coexist in the same frame. Furthermore, the images that originate within the diegetic field immediately propagate; they are intercut with shots of TV viewers at home, all made visually exchangeable by the way they are bathed in a silver-gray light.

One of the effects of the proliferation of points of view the film pursues is a sense of a distributed agency, an effect that prepares for the climactic scene of the revenge of the memorabilia, where inanimate objects behold a critical gaze onto Delacroix. It sets the stage for the possibility that their gaze and their movement will carry the ontological critique of the film, that is, the realization that that the ontology of the object and the thing, rather than the subject and the human, are still the most apt (yet emphatically not the most desirable) to describe both the Black and blackness. It also shows how minutely the film is constructed as a wound-up philosophical toy animated by viewers' desire.

Object movement

The scene of the revenge of the memorabilia is at the philosophical heart of the film because, in this context, the object's faculty to move functions as the mark of the human. Retroactively, the scene is only partially startling because it had been prepared by a progressive reduction of human movement to object movement throughout the film: Delacroix's mechanical gesturing, Manray's tap dancing, Dunwitty's stiff body language, and so on. In other words, the film repeatedly stages a passage from the human to the object so that it can also reverse it and dramatize a passage from the object to the human.

The film suggests that its textual system should be understood as a mechanical object from the very beginning. The first shot of the film focuses on a giant clock/window in Delacroix's sumptuous and light-filled clock-tower loft. Keeping the timepiece in focus, the camera rotates counterclockwise and spirals down to show Delacroix in bed, thus immediately introducing the motif of historical and spatial circularity and recurrence. The direction of the first camera movement suggests a movement "back in time," which eventually leads to the film's deliberate confusion between repetition and remembrance that has prompted Laski to read the film through the idea of trauma.

After the camera reaches ground level and offers a long shot of the room with the clock in the background, Delacroix gets out of bed. The film then cuts to a medium shot of his reflection on the bathroom mirror, shown from behind his back. The image is immediately double, and he is visible from both sides. Rapid cuts show him gingerly and efficiently brushing his teeth, gargling, and then shaving his head. His voice-over begins with the sudden exclamation, "Satire!," and proceeds to list three dictionary definitions of the term, "a: A literary work in which human vice or folly is ridiculed or attacked scornfully; b: the branch of literature that composes such works; c: irony, derision, or caustic wit used to attack or expose folly, vice, or stupidity."

Offering a dictionary definition of satire is a way to preemptively frame the film as an act of critique toward the content it will mobilize, and to do so "objectively," by calling upon a recognized authority in order to remove any ambiguity about the film's intention. Speaking in all earnestness, Lee said that he provided this dictionary definition of the term because "motherfuckers are stupid," a word choice that already implies his foreknowledge that this strategy most likely will not work.

During this morning routine, most of the scene has a predominantly blue décor, and the lighting is harsh. Given how hard it is to lose the blue tint of digital video when it is transferred to film, *Bamboozled* deploys a lot of blue in the sets in order to facilitate such exchange. This lighting design thus also shows a commitment to establishing what will become adventurous scenarios of visual equivalence throughout the film, including the "metallic" silver light that equalizes the characters' different skin tones as they are shown watching the live broadcast of Manray's execution.

Delacroix's stiff, affected, and unnatural delivery of the dictionary definition of satire progressively matches the pace of the music and becomes a form of rapping, anticipating later sequences with the Mau Maus where the film's editing also conforms to the rhythms of a freestyle rap session or a DJ scratching a record. The film then cuts to an eye-level medium shot of Delacroix, with the camera mounted on a dolly moving around the loft clockwise. Now directly addressing the audience, he exclaims: "Bonjour! My name is Pierre Delacroix." There is nothing realistic in his heavy-handed direct address. The frank tone of his speech, his accent, and his affected mannerisms are deliberately artificial and simulacral, that is, they don't care to conform to a real-life referent, and instead produce an effect of hollowness insofar as Delacroix presents a set of bodily motions that appear mechanical rather than soulful. "I am a television writer—a creative person. I am partly responsible for what you see in your idiot box," he continues. The dolly continues to move clockwise and eventually shows the entire loft. There are two giant clock-shaped windows, a feature that adds to the overall sense of repetition and recurrence, especially given that one of them appears to come up behind him even before he has come full circle. They also introduce the motif of the double and create a sense of accelerated time.

Delacroix appears like a mechanical puppet mounted on a train set. One could argue that it is the dolly's movement that is propelling his speech and creating an effect of ventriloquism, as if his voice was coming from somewhere other than his mouth. It anticipates the discovery, at the end of the film, that his entire narration might have been posthumous.

Stevie Wonder's song, "Misrepresented People," plays in the soundtrack in order to directly address questions of representation and cultural legacy. It sets up the dilemma that Lee addressed with the wall of fame in *Do the Right Thing*. But now, Lee is no longer asking, "Why are there no brothers on the wall?" but instead undertaking a reflection on the necessity of mediation, here provided by the satirical framing of the film. In the second episode of the first season of *Chappelle's Show*, Dave Chappelle makes a similar, yet more outrageous, move: "You don't want to hear a young black dude say half of the things that I have been thinking," he says, "it would freak America out." And concludes, "The only way people would listen to the stuff I think is if a pretty white girl sang my thoughts." As a "pretty white girl" comes on stage, Chappelle proceeds to write on index cards, which he then passes to her so she can sing their content. He begins with political statements such as "Crack was invented and distributed to intentionally destroy the black community," or "The police never looked for Tupac and Biggie's murderers," but he quickly turns personal and begins to address her directly, expressing his desire for her, rather than employing her simply as a channel through which to convey his thoughts. Similarly, Lee sets up a clear frame, satire, which depends on some form of critical distance, only to have this distance collapse in the course of the film as the desire for the imagery it unleashes takes hold.

The dolly shot begins and ends with a flare—it is one of the ways the film foregrounds the process of image-making from the beginning. An abrupt cut shows the façade of a squatted building as the camera tilts down to reveal a giant billboard ad for "Da Bomb" Malt Liquor, "125% pure pleasure." As we cut to the inside, the song continues. It's morning and time to go to work. Womack wakes up Manray, and they leave the building. The proliferation of points of view begins here with the fast-paced editing of a variety of unusual shots, including an extremely low angle onto the portable "stage" they are carrying for Manray's street performance—this proliferation acquires coherence only after we hear the sounds of Manray's tapping. From the beginning, the film frames tap dancing as *assemblage art*, that is, art made with an "assembled" musical instrument, which includes the performer, makeshift tap shoes made by sticking beer bottle caps to their soles, and the portable wooden stage on which they will produce the tapping sounds.

A sound bridge leads to Manray and Womack's performance in front of the CNS building. As the editing continues to uphold this sense of proliferated points of view (including shots from the ground, at street level), Womack eventually exclaims, "Don't hurt 'em," referring to Man Ray's feet, or possibly his shoes. Calling attention to the subtle line between exhilaration and pain, body part and prop, Womack also introduces the idea of the interchange between subjects and objects that will become a theme of the film.

Tap dancing has a number of important connections with mechanization and the demands of modern life. It is percussive, like drumming in jazz, with the difference that it is the dancer's body that becomes the instrument: "A great drummer dances sitting down. A great tap-dancer drums standing up."[28] Several synecdoches are at play within the tap dancing "assemblage": the body of the dancer performs like a percussive instrument, and the feet stand for the head, but also substitute for a drummer's hands. In this relationship between part and whole, animate and inanimate, the passage from subject to object occurs because the dancer is turned into a prosthesis of himself. Tapping can also be seen as a form of "sound writing" that connects the dancer more explicitly to automated human movements, such as typewriting, and to machines that write with sound, such as the telegraph, with which it has been historically associated.[29] Tap dancing engenders a rich multimodal sensorial experience because of the way its typewriter-like sounds punctuate the unfolding of filmic temporality. They act as diegetic reminders of the effaced mechanics of the cinematic apparatus. Because these mechanical sounds may appear to *generate* the movements of the film image, tap's "machinic" quality brings the dancer very close to the automaton.

Overall, *Bamboozled*'s two opening sequences already set up the experience of mechanical movement as it applies to the set, the characters, and the editing. They do so by pursuing three lineages of the machinic. The first is the already mentioned relationship between the tap dancer and the automaton, the mechanical toy popular in the early 1700s, which constituted an important prototype of the mechanically reproduced image by doing what André Bazin has identified as the main aspiration of the photographic image: representation of life via reproduction of life.[30]

The second lineage connects the automaton to slave labor, an association that was frequently discussed at the time of the convergence of technologies of sound reproduction (the gramophone) and intellectual property law. Even before that, the slave-as-automaton was featured in Barnum's theater as one of his first displays (it was, therefore, arguably at the beginning of American popular culture). Barnum acquired the right to exhibit a slave woman, Joice Heath, who was said to have been George Washington's mammy and was allegedly 161 years old. The ruse Barnum pursued, however, was the suggestion that she was not a woman at all, but rather an automaton, a machine.[31] In *Bamboozled*, this lineage returns in the several encounters between Manray and Womack and in the media image of previous artists performing machinic movements, such as Mantan Moreland in *The Gray Ghost*.

The third lineage refers to the relationship between the performing black diegetic body and the cinematic apparatus. Maurice has shown how early talkies relied on the "black voice" to resolve the problem of sound/image synchronization because of its implied synesthesia, that is, the fact that "black voice" describes a sound that has the ability to deliver a matching image. Early talkies turned to black performers because the black body both corporealized the apparatus and provided it with a sense of reconciled wholeness. Tap, however, is also capable of achieving the opposite effect—machinic disarticulation. "Through the mobilization and suspension of beats in different areas of the body, . . . a torso appears to *listen* to a leg, a forearm *summons* a beat from a waist and responds with its own."[32] Using animistic language, Brooks describes the disarticulation of the body that the tap dancer is required to master: the torso *listens*, the forearm *summons*. Through this disarticulation, the dancer can produce a rhythmic and bodily equivalent of the dissemination of points of view that commodity fetishism creates in the film. By interpreting the machinic as the sign/affect of the commodity, this animism institutes the same fetishism that places "eyes everywhere."

Disarticulation also creates the possibility of multiple temporalities, particularly in the dance Manray performs at the last taping of the show, when he refuses to blacken up—"I am not playing myself no more," he explains to Delacroix—and comes on stage without blackface. He delivers a monologue that reverses the one featured in *Mantan*'s pilot, urging the audience to go to their windows and yell out "I am sick and tired of being a nigger and I can't take it anymore," before falling back onto the stage. After a few moments of stillness, he gets up and begins to tap at maddening speed. His movements are so fast that they appear as "a series of brush strokes" and "gashes of color," as Brooks describes them, as if the image was being scarred by the speed of a body with which it can no longer keep up. As Fanon put it, "The black man is a toy in the white man's hands. So, in order to break the vicious cycle, he explodes."[33] Similarly, Manray is tapping himself out of the deadening and reifying beat of minstrel dance.

Manray's final "Dance of Death" continues this synthesis between the human and the automaton by framing it more clearly as a "scene of subjection." A barrage of bullets fired by the Mau Maus "winds him up" like a toy, and this animatedness reenacts scenes of coerced movement in slave narratives; this recalls not just slave labor but, more perversely, the seemingly carefree movements that the minstrel show is supposedly portraying, such as the slaves dancing in their quarters or the moment the master tells the slave, "Now, dance!" It also harkens back to the "battle royal" episode from Ralph Ellison's *Invisible Man*, when the protagonist is forced to box blindfolded before retrieving his compensation—coins and a few crumpled bills tossed by the "prominent citizens" who comprise his audience—from an electrified rug. Rendering the body's movement as a twitch speaks both to the compulsory association of blackness with coerced performance (rather than apparently free-spirited self-expression, a la Topsy) and to the muscular spasm that Fanon identifies as the outcome of the inability for the colonized to act out.

Finally, the machinic extends to the editing pattern of the film itself. As I have been suggesting throughout, *Bamboozled* progresses in fits and spurts, eventually glitching and stuttering on a variety of occasions: a repeated, partially overlapping editing is reserved for the fantasies that Delacroix does not act on (for example, when he imagines slapping Dunwitty for repeating the N-word) or is used to express his frustration (as when he confronts Dunwitty and the show's director, Jukka, about unauthorized changes to the tone of the show; here, he sighs loudly with frustration, throwing his hands up in the air— a movement that is shown twice from two different angles).

Most of the time, the editing structure conforms to a generalized sense of object movement, but it sometimes appears inspired by a specific object that is internal to, or implied by, a specific scene. The scene where the Mau Maus resolve to take action against *Mantan* takes place in a pool hall and begins with Mos Def's character Big Blak Afrika entering from a door visible in the back. He is upset and blurts out, "This Manray is fucking it up for the whole fucking . . ." but cannot finish his sentence. His hands are flailing. Then, the Mau Maus are all huddled around the pool table, and Big Blak Afrika suddenly asks, "You know what I'm sayin'?" Rather than eliciting an answer, this question initiates a call-and-response, where virtually every Mau Mau repeats the same question, with the editing cutting to the location of each repetition, thus mimicking a pool ball bouncing off the sides of the table. From a sonic standpoint, however, the editing mimics the "scratching" of a record, thus establishing another form of stuttering and partial repetition. Eventually, 1/16th throws his hands up in the air and says "No!," arresting this movement. The scene concludes with a decision to act. Big Blak Afrika again prods, "This shit is got to be big. It's going to have some symbolism to it. Like John Carlos and Tommie Smith at the 1968 Olympics." The film then cuts to a clip of the original footage showing the two athletes bowing their heads and raising their fists in the Black Power salute.

With so many characters and editing patterns associated with mechanical movement—including Dunwitty's deployment of black vernacular street language and gestures, which are just as stiff as Delacroix's "buppy" demeanor—moments of "naturalistic" acting in the film call attention to themselves—for example, the scene where Womack communicates to Manray that he is leaving the show. The two are shot against a large window. Womack, who is comparatively darker skinned, appears like a silhouette. "The New Millennium, ah? It's the same bullshit done over again," he tells Manray. He then turns around and passes his hand over his face like a curtain to signal a transition into the part of the "coon": "Yessum . . . I'll coon for you. Anything to make you feel better, Massa." Then, still in character, he picks up his suitcase and leaves. I don't intend to suggest that the "coon" is an example of naturalistic acting, but rather that, by refusing to cut, the scene underlines the human skills and craft required to perform this part. This flaunted seamless transition offers a real-time example of coerced mimeticism.

The primary conceit of the film—that is, that it arranges itself as a wound-up philosophical toy propelled by viewers' desire—is so pervasive that, by the time we reach the final sequence, the montage of clips from film and television history feels like an automated barrage of images flowing out of the film's own wounded mechanical body. From the beginning, this filmic-mechanical body has been primarily, although not exclusively, equated with Delacroix's body. The discovery of his posthumous narration, inspired by *Sunset Boulevard* (Billy Wilder, 1950), strengthens the hauntological and traumatic bent of the film. Access to the primal scene of subjection is foreclosed by its traumatic nature, but this scene will nevertheless continue to repeat itself. The final montage presents images that feel like *déjà vu*, either because they echo moments or situations we have already seen in the film or because of their uncanny familiarity with countless other media images. The film takes on what we can describe as a stratigraphic approach to the image archive in the sense of showing how, underneath an image, there are countless other similar images; such an approach strengthens the recursive temporality and hauntological sensibility of the film.

In the last sequence, a distraught Sloan visits Delacroix in his office. The set is pitch-black, and Delacroix is wearing blackface. At gunpoint, Sloan demands that he play the tape she has made for him. He complies. As the tape begins to play, she chastises him, "Look at what you have contributed to." We have seen this layering of images in the background of the action before, but its repetition now gives the sense that this media imagery constantly surrounds us. He asks for her gun, but she accidentally shoots him and then leaves. *Amos 'n' Andy* is playing in the background. Surprisingly, Delacroix's voice-over resumes with the usual incongruous tone: "As I bled to death, as life oozed out of my body, I was reminded of something the great poet James Baldwin said: 'People pay for what they do and even more for what they have allowed themselves to become, and they pay for it simply by the lives they live.' Goodbye cousins. Please tune in again next week for *Mantan: The New Millennium Minstrel Show*." Delacroix's request suggests that what we have just watched might in fact be the show's rerun; thus, the viewer becomes part of this apparently endless cycle of production, reproduction, and repetition.[34]

The cut to the TV set that begins the archival sequence proper occurs in mid-sentence (between "*New Millennium*" and "*Minstrel Show*") thus connecting his oozing body to the outpour of racism that is about to appear on the screen. Initially, Delacroix's dark profile is in the bottom right corner of the frame, but he slowly falls backwards and off the frame as a clip with Stepin Fetchit begins to play. After the next cut, the TV image fills the frame completely.

Lee has said that he "always wanted to end the film with a heritage that would be a culmination of the most racist scenes in film and television, as a summation."[35] Sam Pollard, who edited the montage to match this heritage to the length of Terrence Blanchard's orchestral score, synched together the clips by maintaining consistency of movement and pace. Occasionally, the orchestral score subsides, and we hear the diegetic lines of dialog—for example, in a clip from *Song of the South* (Wilfred Jackson and Harve Foster, 1946) and in a series of clips featuring black male and female characters in servile roles, saying "yessum" and "yessir," which concludes the montage. Often, the dialog creates sound bridges that carry over to more instances of the same racist trope. There is a section on tap dancing that includes a clip from *Dimples* (William A. Seiter, 1936), featuring Shirley Temple tapping with two dancers in blackface, in front of an audience also in blackface; a section on excessive eating, which includes footage from a watermelon eating contest; a series of chaotic movements and interactions with out-of-control vehicles where blacks are ridiculed for their ineptitude toward machinery, which offers a chaotic spectacle of thoughtless movement. This sequence flows into the next section on grotesque eyes seemingly outgrowing the face, as if they were possessed by an independent agency.

This idea of uncontrollable growth connects to the sense of the constitutive incontinence of the black body. Through this reverse synecdoche whereby the part takes over the whole, the rest of the body loses any sense of intentionality and becomes akin to brute matter. A section on excessively open mouths references ideas of blackness as a bottomless hole. There is a segment on objectification and object movement featuring Mantan Moreland jerking uncontrollably on the floor, but there is also footage of a man lying on the ground holding a golf ball with his mouth. The club is swung, and, before it touches the ball, the ball disappears in the man's mouth. A section on white actors in blackface immediately follows: Al Jolson in *The Jazz Singer* (Alan Crosland, 1927) while addressing his Mammy with open arms (one of the moments of synchronized sound in the film), followed by other entertainers, such as Judy Garland, Bing Crosby, and Mickey Rooney, among others, begrudgingly or gingerly putting burnt-cork makeup on their face. There is a clip of Gus from *The Birth of a Nation* (D. W. Griffith, 1915) as the prototypical black rapist, along with a clip where Stepin Fetchit effortlessly jumps over a wooden plank being carried by two men across the set. (The point of listing these clips, albeit summarily, is to reinforce the sense of quantity and diversity exhibited by the themes and tropes featured in this archive of media racism.)

Stepin Fetchit, who rose to popularity during the transition to the sound era, was particularly beloved by critics precisely for the sense of integrity his movements brought to the cinematic image. Maurice has shown how the sense of "wholeness" of African American performances was able to conceal the difficulties of sound synchronization, that is, the fact that it required a fairly static camera, which was a step back from the mobility the camera had achieved at the end of the silent period. She identifies two rhetorical strategies at work in the transition to sound: "Emphasizing the hyper-presence of black bodies in order to deflect attention *away* from the apparatus and using those same bodies and their 'inherent' talents to show off the prowess of the apparatus."[36] Just like the "black voice" reconciles sound with image, the performing black body reconciles the cinematic apparatus with the moving image's aspiration to be lifelike, that is, to move in a life*like* manner. Here the racial fetish coincides with the cinematic fetish. Racial characteristics bring fullness to the imaginary signifier by covering over what is missing: synthesis of sound and image or the actual bodies we only see *as* images.

Wading through

It is almost universally recognized that watching *Bamboozled* is a challenging, if not predominantly displeasing, experience. The film is so relentless and affectively charged that spectators of all races struggle to find a language to describe the way it weighs upon them. The film is obstinately extreme and constantly displays excessive passion.[37] Several essays highlight its frightening "entropic" structure, whereby the film either implodes or explodes (or both, as discussed in one essay) or produces a "tidal wave of undifferentiated images."[38] For these critics, "undifferentiation" is equally descriptive of the interchangeability between images, things, and people already discussed here and of the difficulty for the viewer to disentangle herself from what she is seeing. The film's ability to produce an effect of presence is in this case absolutely overwhelming.

To express the feeling of being submerged in an abject substance, Kara Keeling writes that watching *Bamboozled* is like "wading through a pool of shit."[39] Yet, as I have shown, the film's own construction (as a wound-up toy set in motion by audiences' desires) reveals the viewer's complicity in creating this uncomfortable sense of material density, while imagery of extraction and secretion produce a fraught ambiguity about the origin of this matter. In fact, the very reading I have provided by focusing on the idea of object movement is only possible after repeatedly wading through the film. Its mechanics are hidden underneath a layer of muck. With this effect, *Bamboozled* exposes both the melancholic relation that attaches America to its others and the introjection of this same relation by the melancholic object—the ingestion of its own inassimilability.

While eating the other, America eats itself. While attempting to expel it, it finds itself covered in shit.

Yet it is difficult to produce a smoking gun or point to a specific moment in which this affective response is produced. Most scholarship consistently attributes these complex and troubling responses to the accumulation of racist imagery, an accumulation that is so relentless that it seemingly acquires a material density. But, it might also be an effect of the specific ways in which the film plays with the question of its *proximity* to contemporary culture; in other words, *Bamboozled* poses a "what if?" that is difficult to ignore. Critical reactions to the film indicate a certain amount of confusion about when and where it takes place. Amy Taubin, for example, believes the dance of death occurred either in cyberspace or someone's psyche.[40] The film's assumptions are so far-fetched that it appears absurd and impossible, yet, even though no network would ever think of airing a minstrel show, *COPS* (Junebug's "favorite black show") has been airing for years.

In this sense, *Bamboozled* presents traits of "near-future" fiction, a term that Kalí Tal used to describe Ralph Ellison's *Invisible Man,* John Williams's *The Man Who Cried I Am*, Sam Greenlee's 1966 novel *The Spook Who Sat by the Door*, and Ivan Dixon's 1973 adaptation of it, and other African American narratives that have qualities of futurism and proximity at the same time.[41] Whether they are describing the federal government's conspiracy to exterminate African Americans or black Chicago gangs learning guerrilla techniques from a former CIA agent to ignite an armed revolution across the United States, these fictional worlds can be almost perfectly juxtaposed to our real world except for the resultant courses of events that emerge from the fiction. The fictional outcomes might feel implausible in some ways, but they are also the logical conclusions from the premises that these fictional worlds share with ours. So, there is a hypothetical quality to these narratives, but they are not counterfactual in the sense of imagining an inverted equivalent of our world; they therefore cannot be successfully placed at a distance or resolved on a purely formal level. Instead, these "what if?" scenarios strike very close to home.

Another way of thinking about proximity is by pursuing the question of where *Bamboozled* takes place in relation to the screen. One of the motivations for wading through the film enough times to uncover its organization—again, it can be understood as a mechanical toy moved by audience desires— is to show how its blackness is made in cooperation with the audience and to uncover the remarkable density that this blackness acquires in the process of its own making. Blackness is never merely onscreen but is built in the interaction with the screen—just like blackface is cooperatively conceived across Dunwitty's long conference table during Delacroix's pitch or built by the studio audience's interaction with the minstrel show.

This interactivity is particularly evident if we take Kara Keeling's position that the processes that we use to understand cinematic reality are the same processes that we use to understand our world. Following Gilles Deleuze, Keeling argues that the cinema is part of, rather than distinct from, reality because the processes of perception and affection that are mobilized by the cinema are not exclusive to it but are instead generalized in culture and society through the invention and spread of moving image technologies. This is why cinematic perception is implicated in the production and reproduction of social reality. Thus, the way blackness is perceived in the world is already cinematic because the cinematic has already organized perception. Said otherwise, *as* image, blackness is the paradigm for the cinematic image. Every appearance of a black body is recognized as an appearance of the Black—a cliché but also *common sense*— because of the collective process of connecting perceptions in the present with "experiences, knowledges, traditions" as memory-images from the past.[42]

Bamboozled is very effective in creating this image of common sense. Our realization at the end of the film that we have been dancing with it all along—moving it just like

Delacroix activates the Jolly Nigger bank—strengthens the idea that there is no clear distinction between the cinematic and the world. The cinema is part of the world, and it informs the way we understand the world. So, we can rethink or rephrase Spike Lee's claim that he wanted to explore the power of images in *Bamboozled*. We can also think of the film as a commitment to understanding how common sense is created, that is, how images are formed *commonly*. Certainly, images are formed in the commons because of the synergy and interaction between media and reality, but images also emerge through a perception in the present and the memory of perceptions from the past; further, images come about because of the interactions between media and their spectator, and spectators with one another— the latter as exemplified in the studio audience's reaction to the minstrel show. The frightening realization that the final montage makes available, then, is the fact that those images exist for the simple reason that the public likes them. They exist because of us, not because of Spike Lee.

Notes

1   Gary Crowdus and Dan Georgakas, "Thinking about the Power of Images: An Interview with Spike Lee," *Cineaste* 26, no. 2 (2001): 9.

2   Besides the essays cited throughout, see W. J. T. Mitchell, "Living Color: Race, Stereotype, and Animation in Spike Lee's *Bamboozled*," *What Do Pictures Want? The Lives and Loves of Images* (Chicago: University of Chicago Press, 2005); Harry J. Elam, Jr., "Spike Lee's *Bamboozled*," in *Black Cultural Traffic: Crossroads in Global Performance and Popular Culture*, ed. Harry J. Elam, Jr. and Jackson Kennell (Ann Arbor: University of Michigan Press, 2005); Beretta Smith-Shomade, "'I Be Smakin' My Hoes': Paradox and Authenticity in *Bamboozled*," in *The Spike Lee Reader*, ed. Paula J. Massood (Philadelphia: Temple, 2007); Susan Gubar, "Racial Camp in *The Producers* and *Bamboozled*," *Film Quarterly* 60, no. 2 (2006): 26–37.

3 It is part of the commonsensical nature of stereotypes to be almost "objective" and easily recognizable; yet, as the pedagogical exercise performed with Toni Morrison's "Recitatif" shows, the identification of stereotypes requires active reading and therefore can produce different results with each individual. That said, my goal is not to be exhaustive but only exemplary, and for pedagogical purposes, it is more important to set the process in motion than to secure unequivocal results.

4 Cynthia Lucia, "Race, Media, and Money: A Critical Symposium on Spike Lee's *Bamboozled*," *Cineaste* 26, no. 2 (2001): 10.

5 Stephen Best, *The Fugitive's Properties: Law and the Poetics of Possession* (Chicago and London: University of Chicago Press, 2004), Ch. 2.

6 Zeinabu Irene Davis, "'Beautiful-ugly' Blackface: An Esthetic Appreciation of *Bamboozled*," *Cineaste* 26, no. 2 (2001): 17.

7 Ed Guerrero, *Do the Right Thing* (London: BFI, 2001), 53.

8 Alice Maurice, "From New Deal to No Deal: Blackface Minstrelsy, *Bamboozled*, and Reality Television," in *Burnt Cork: Traditions and Legacies of Blackface Minstrelsy*, ed. Stephen Johnson (Amherst: University of Massachusetts Press, 2012), 193.

9 Emphasis added. Stanley Crouch, Eric Lott, Margo Jefferson, and Michele Wallace, "Minding the Messenger: A Symposium on *Bamboozled*," *Black Renaissance Noire* 3, no. 3 (2001): 6–7; Armond White, "Post-Art Minstrelsy," *Cineaste* 26, no. 2 (2001): 12–13.

10 Manthia Diawara, "The Blackface Stereotype," in *Blackface*, ed. David Levinthal (Santa Fe, NM: Arena Editions, 1999), 15.

11 Greg Tate, "*Bamboozled*: White Supremacy and a Black Way of Being Human," *Cineaste* 26, no. 2 (2001): 16.

12 Phil Chiedester, Shannon Campbell, and Jamel Bell, "'Black is Blak': *Bamboozled* and the Crisis of a Postmodern Racial Identity," *The Howard Journal of Communications* 17 (2006): 289.

13 Linda Williams, *Playing the Race Card: Melodramas of Black and White from Uncle Tom to O.J. Simpson* (Princeton and Oxford: Princeton University Press, 2001).

14 This idea of "secretion" is partly inspired by Jacqueline Goldsby's *A Spectacular Secret: Lynching in American Life and Literature* (Chicago: University of Chicago Press, 2006).

15 Arthur Knight, *Disintegrating the Musical: Black Performance and American Musical Film* (Durham, NC: Duke University Press, 2002), 243 and 110–19. The "Bum Garage" routine is performed by Flournoy Miller and Johnnie Lee.

16 Technically, this is Derridian *différance*, the neologism he created by substituting the letter "e" in "difference" with the letter "a," in order to apply difference to the signifier itself. By changing a letter without changing the sound of the word Derrida combines together the concept of *differing* and *deferring*. Similarly, Henry Louis Gates seeks a typographic way to indicate how black vernacular language and literary tradition apply difference to its standard English counterpart. Henry Louis Gates, *The Signifying Monkey* (New York: Oxford University Press, 1988), 44–51; Jacques Derrida, "Différance," in *The Margins of Philosophy*, trans. Alan Bass (Chicago: University of Chicago Press, 1982), 3–27.

17 Lee recognized that putting on the blackface makeup was devastating for Tommy Davidson and Savion Glover; it took away part of their souls and their manhood and made them think about Bert Williams, who had to do that his entire career. Crowdus and Georgakas, "Thinking about the Power of Images," 6.

18 Ed Guerrero, "*Bamboozled*: In the Mirror of Abjection," in *Black Contemporary American Cinema: Race, Gender and Sexuality at the Movies*, ed. Mia Mask (New York: Routledge, 2012), 109–27.

19 Gregory Laski, "Falling Back into History: The Uncanny Trauma of Blackface Minstrelsy in Spike Lee's *Bamboozled*," *Callaloo* 33, no. 4 (2010): 1102.

20 Kara Keeling, "Passing for Human: *Bamboozled* and Digital Humanism," *Women & Performance: A Journal of Feminist Theory* 15, no. 1 (2005): 244.

21 Tavia Nyong'o, "Unburdening Representation," *The Black Scholar* 44, no. 2 (2014): 75.

22 Among these still shots of the objects there is also a view of Michael Ray Charles's painting titled "Bamboozled," which

features a blackface board game—thus deliberately presenting itself between a picture and a concrete object. The painting belongs to Spike Lee's personal collection

23 Bill Brown, "Reification, Reanimation, and the American Uncanny," *Critical Inquiry* 32 (2006): 175–207.

24 Jennifer Barker, *The Tactile Eye: Touch and the Cinematic Experience* (Berkeley: University of California Press, 2009).

25 *Bamboozled* is dedicated to Budd Schulberg, the screenwriter of *A Face in the Crowd*. For the idea of the tearjerker, see Linda Williams, "Body Genres," *Film Quarterly* 44, no. 4 (1991): 2–13.

26 Maurice, "From New Deal to No Deal," 206–07.

27 Crowdus et al., "Thinking about the Power of Images," 9.

28 Jacqui Malone, *Steppin' on the Blues: The Visible Rhythms of African American Dance* (Urbana and Chicago: University of Illinois Press, 1996), 94–95, cited in Jodi Brooks, "Ghosting the Machine: The Sounds of Tap and the Sounds of Film," *Screen* 44, no. 4 (2003): 363.

29 The African American origins of tap dancing belong to the racial unconscious of the classical Hollywood musical, which, however, displaced these origins and subordinated tapping to the comfort of song and lyrics. See Carol Clover, "Dancin' in the Rain," *Critical Inquiry* 21, no. 4 (1995): 722–47. Jazz similarly bears on the racial unconscious of *noir*. See Eric Lott "The Whiteness of Film Noir," *American Literary History* 9, no. 3 (1997): 542–66; and Dan Flory, *Philosophy, Black Film, Film Noir* (University Park: Penn State Press, 2008).

30 André Bazin, *What Is Cinema? Vol. 1*, trans. Hugh Gray (Berkeley: University of California Press, 1967); Pasi Väliaho, *Mapping the Moving Image: Gesture, Thought and Cinema Circa 1900* (Amsterdam: Amsterdam University Press, 2010).

31 Louis Chude-Sokei, "The Uncanny History of Minstrels and Machines, 1835–1923," in *Burnt Cork: Traditions and Legacies of Blackface Minstrelsy*, ed. Stephen Johnson (Amherst: University of Massachusetts Press, 2012), 104–32.

32 Brooks, "Ghosting the Machine," 370 (my emphasis).

33 Franz Fanon, *Black Skins, White Masks*, trans. Richard Philcox (New York: Grove Press, 2008), 119.

34 Laski, "Falling Back into History," 1107.

35 Spike Lee, *Bamboozled* (Spike Lee, 2000), DVD commentary.

36 Alice Maurice, *The Cinema and Its Shadow: Race and Technology in Early Cinema* (Minneapolis and London: University of Minnesota Press, 2013), 167.

37 Todd McGowan, *Spike Lee* (Urbana: University of Illinois Press, 2014), 128.

38 Chiedester, "Black is Blak," 299.

39 Keeling, "Passing for Human," 243.

40 Amy Taubin, "Spike Lee's Own Scary Movie," *The Village Voice*, Tuesday, October 3, 2000, http://www.villagevoice.com/film/spike-lees-own-scary-movie-6417368. Accessed on May 10, 2015.

41 Kalí Tal, "That Just Kills Me: Black Militant Near-Future Fiction," *Social Text* 20, no. 2 (2002): 65–91.

42 Kara Keeling, *The Witch's Flight: The Cinematic, the Black Femme, and the Image of Common Sense* (Durham, NC: Duke University Press, 2007), 14.

CONCLUSION

How to perform a critical race analysis

The purpose of this book has been to conceptualize how concerns addressed within Critical Race Theory can provide tools of formal analysis to be employed in film studies. The book's narrative has drawn from three bodies of scholarship on race—legal studies, critical theory (broadly understood), and black studies—and intertwined these fields around a series of questions. These queries deal with the relationship between formal equality and social equality; the connections among color blindness as a legal category, color blindness as a visual possibility, and the (visual) fact of blackness; the relationship between political and aesthetic representation as they combine in the "burden of representation" bestowed on minority art; and finally, the relationship between photographic ontology and the visual fact of blackness, including the way issues of stillness and movement across technologies of visual media affect the visibility of the human subject, the full citizen. While developing this narrative, the book has offered several ways of thinking about how race and blackness are legally, sensorially, aesthetically, affectively, and performatively made in the context of the eroticism of everyday racial encounters with people and things.

Critical Race Theory's more radical project puts race at the heart of humanistic inquiry in order to address how it affects the very concept and boundaries of the human subject. This book offers tools to continue this project. Further, this book is inspired by the idea that the afterlife of slavery haunts the aesthetics and form of the law while also besetting media texts and influencing the way the black body is (still) often encountered in the field of vision. In this way, the book has remained attentive to the question of the ontology of blackness as it concerns both the political ontology of the Black—as subject vs. object, human vs. nonhuman, commodity vs. individual—and of *blackness* as such, which, as *Bamboozled* displays with extraordinary clarity, is still too dangerously close to the ontology of the thing.

This conclusion offers some suggestions for how the "critical race analysis" developed in this book might approach film and popular culture texts that address some of these issues through narrative, aesthetics, or form. I will then tease out some of the implications of reading *Bamboozled* as a text that contributes to the inquiry of Critical Race Theory; in particular, the film highlights the relationship between the mobility that blackness acquires in the process of being made and the repercussions that the "making" of blackness has on the question of representation.

The counterfactual form is one of the earliest ways in which the cinema reflected on the issue of equality; this form can be found in films pivoting around the imagination of an inverted world such as *White Man's Burden* (Desmond Nakano, 1995) or *Suture* (Scott McGehee and David Siegel, 1993). When approaching these films from the point of view of formal equality, one might begin by examining whether or not they succeed in also fostering a scenario of social equality and whether they unfold from the point of view of whiteness constructed as the injured position, as happens in *White Man's Burden*.

In *Suture*—a film that employs formal equality to its extreme in order to criticize color blindness as a viable premise for equality—it is the form of the counterfactual that is the object of investigation. *Suture* is ostensibly a film about a case of mistaken identity between two characters who are treated as if they were visually identical within the diegesis. Yet, these characters are played by a white and black actor, respectively, Michael Harris (Vincent) and Dennis Haysbert (Clay). Shot in black and white, the film presents a relentlessly polarized visual scheme that offers the spectator a visual difference between the two characters that the film's diegesis disavows, since no one in the film appears to realize that the two half-brothers look nothing alike. The diegesis is color-blind but the viewers cannot be.

Suture can be read as the counterpart to Toni Morrison's "Recitatif" because of the way the latter creates a world where the characters see one another, yet the reader is *kept blind* as to their identity. *Suture* pursues the opposite scenario. The viewer is constantly asked to imagine a visual identity between a black actor and a white actor that the image does not provide. Hence, the film critiques the assumed formal equality of color blindness by creating an impossible spectatorial position where the viewer has to constantly disavow what she sees. Building on high-contrast black-and-white cinematography, the film creates a visual grid wherein Clay's blackness is not meant to index race but is instead deployed as a pure signifier of difference in a Saussurian fashion. Yet, even at the visual level, actor Dennis Haysbert *as* Clay does not exchange equally for actor Michael Harris *as* Vincent. Still, the viewer strives to have someone from the diegetic world avow her visual apprehension; she longs to have the difference she sees affirmed by the characters. Ultimately, by emphasizing its unequal exchange, *Suture* mocks the formal equality of counterfactual logic while showing the impossibility of a truly color-blind viewing position.

Chappelle's Show is an example of effective use of the counterfactual form because it is initiated from the point of view of the underprivileged position; it thus vindicates CRT's defense of the epistemic advantage of the point of view of the oppressed. For example, a sketch called "Tron Carter's 'Law & Order' (Uncensored)" features a "run through" of an inverted justice system where the sudden police raid of a white

CEO's mansion is announced by a hand grenade rolling onto his bedroom floor. Police interrogation is conducted without any regard for his civil rights, his attorney is overworked and unprepared, and he is sentenced to life in prison without any explanation of his crime. On the other hand, Tron Carter, a black crack cocaine dealer, receives an apologetic phone call from the local police precinct alerting him to trafficking charges against him that, unfortunately, have to be addressed. Carter agrees to turn himself in a few days later, between 2:00 and 6:00 p.m., but shows up at midnight and is welcomed with a beautiful spread of fruits and cheeses in order to discuss how to make sure that this situation will not embarrass him in front of his community. *Chappelle's Show* has countless examples of this type of counterfactual, including the notorious inaugural sketch that provides a biting critique of the very idea of color blindness—taken literally, the sketch produces a black Klan leader who, because he is blind, does not know he is black.

C.S.A: *Confederate States of America* (Kevin Willmott, 2004) employs the counterfactual as its premise: the South won the Civil War and, in the Confederate States of America, slavery is still legal. This is a powerful enough assumption, but it can also be quickly dismissed. Thus, the film's strongest critique comes from its enactments of formal and aesthetic passing. *C.S.A.* opens abruptly with a commercial for a life insurance company broadcast by the fictional TV channel in San Francisco that is showing a controversial British documentary critical of the Confederate States of America. The viewer, however, does not know that this is the framing of the film, and the discovery is shocking. The commercial introduces a man sitting on a sunny porch while the voice-over says, "A man fills many roles in his lifetime: provider, protector, master of the house." After the man helps a little girl who has fallen from her bicycle, the voice-over continues "Because, no matter what they call you, at the end of the day, you know you are just dad." Then comes the punch line: "Confederate Family insurance. For over 100 years, protecting people and their property." This last word coincides with a pan to the right that reveals a black youth trimming the bushes on the grounds of what we now understand to be a plantation house.

Only retroactively, from the point of view of this pan shot, do we realize that there was nothing in the form or aesthetics of the commercial that would suggest the direction it was going to take. Instead, it had all the markers of the "genre": soft-focus cinematography strangely appropriate for the subject matter, a setting indicative of wealth to be protected and passed along to future generations, the default whiteness of the subject to whom the commercial is addressed, and the usual empty rhetoric of capitalist realism. Other conditions being equal, all of this would have made the association between "master of the house" and "dad" generically quite benign (even though outrageous from the point of view of gender politics).

C.S.A., which coincides with the broadcast of the British documentary, is interrupted by commercials every ten minutes or so. Thus, the entire film could be watched from the point of view of the commercials—which ultimately means from the point of view of the commodity and, in this scenario, the slave. The commercials advertise actual products that were somewhat recently discontinued such as Gold Dust Twins (1880s–1930s), Darkie Toothpaste (1900s–1980s), and Niggerhair Tobacco (1870s–1950s). Or, these ads reference actual historical figures, as in the spot for The Cartwright Institute—named after Dr. Samuel Cartwright who, in 1851, wrote "Diseases and Peculiarities of the Negro Race"—for "the study of freedom illnesses, such as drapetomania, rascality, and negritude." Predictably, there is also an ad for a reality show that looks like *COPS* but is called *Runaway* instead.

Even more than in *Bamboozled*, it is the *passing* for real commercials that carries the most effective critique. This is because such passing unearths a too-recent history of the exploitation of blackness in commodity culture and reveals the property relations usually concealed underneath the benign patina of the advertisements being mimicked. Similar to *Bamboozled*, the commercials introduce an uncanny temporality that refers both to a near past when some of the products were still in use and, oddly, to a near future when a generalized pathologization of blackness continues to increase—of course, the film critiques both.

Passing often reproduces the confusion between *equation* and *equality*, but this is not always the case. In films such as Wendell B. Harris's *Chameleon Street* (1989) or Anna Deavere's Smith's *Twilight: Los Angeles* (2000), it is the black body *as black* that performs the act of passing. What happens when passing is framed as an enactment of blackness, rather than whiteness? How does the *form* of passing function as a critique of ideas of authenticity? Or, in the case of Deavere Smith's film—a one-woman reenactment of testimony from about forty among the two hundred witnesses she interviewed in the wake of the Rodney King riots—how does a black body come to transcend its particularity and manage to express a number of other bodies?

Chameleon Street is based on the true story of Douglas Street, who performed a series of successful impersonations including a sports reporter, a physician, a lawyer, and a medical student. The filmmaker, Wendell B. Harris, became interested in Street's ability to make his interlocutors believe in whatever he was passing as. Michael Gillespie argues that Street's passing is not implicated in the "ontological violation" that occurs in passing for white but needs to be understood instead as an enactment of the performative possibilities of blackness.[1] Even though conning is not racially specific, Street's blackness is in this case instrumental to his ability to "act convincingly." Because blackness comes with the expectation of integrity— that is, the idea that skin color somehow matches identity and that identity is perfectly transparent and intelligible from the outside—Street persuades his audience through his ability to produce the illusion of the perfect "black image."

His impersonations are neither instrumental to the acquisition of privilege or wealth, nor are they symptoms of self-hatred. Instead, they pursue constant reinvention and an unbound performativity as empowering for its own sake. Gillespie observes how Street embodies the vision that

Ralph Ellison had for the character of Rinehart, the unseen conman for whom the invisible man is constantly mistaken. Ellison described Rinehart as the personification of chaos and the embodiment of what the preacher's sermon in the book's prologue already outlines: black is, black ain't. Blackness is a process, a constant beginning, invention, and reinvention. Passing, therefore, does not have to measure up to any kind of authentic black essence, but it can invent and create something new.

Retroactively, *Chameleon Street* can shed light on another quality of Morrison's "Recitatif," that is, the fact that the way she structured the text has also enabled her to grant a similar performativity to her characters. In fact, Twyla and Roberta can pass from one racial identity to the other within Morrison's text, regardless of what the narrative says. Consider the exercise I offered for this text in Chapter One: when we interpret a specific descriptor as racial, and we match it up with the character to whom it is attributed as a way to pin down her racial identity, all we will see is the characters' constant movement, their endless passing, from the "white" to the "black" column and vice versa.

This performativity is specifically racial because blackness comes with the expectation of integrity—an expectation that takes different forms in different media and genres and is rehearsed at the end of *Chameleon Street* in the way the film handles the popular story of the Scorpion and the Frog. Several characters from the film narrate a segment of the story as they look into the camera. Each segment takes on the color, inflection, and "spin" that each character gives it—more gothic, more suspenseful, more dramatic, more self-indulgent—and each delivery and version of the story encourages the attribution of a specific personality to the character—here is the drama queen, here is the privileged white dude, here is the gay character—and so on. The story ends with the scorpion stinging the frog and both of them drowning while the frog asks the scorpion why he has stung her, to which he usually replies, "Because it's in my nature." However, in *Chameleon Street*, Douglas Street, who delivers the closing line, substitutes the term "nature" with "character": "Because it is in my character," he says. There is no nature or essence that can explain the reasons for his performances, no nature or essence by which he has to abide. We will not find the integrity between image and identity that blackness is supposed to deliver. Instead, we are left with the endless play of performativity—playing for its own sake, playing for freedom.[2]

Anna Deavere Smith's passing is similar to Street's in the sense that it is entirely performative, yet it does not entail any impersonation. Smith's theater technique is based on absolutely precise reenactments of segments from interviews she carries out with people who have suffered situations of extreme racial strife. Her two best-known pieces are *Fires in the Mirror* (George C. Wolfe, 1993), about the Crown Heights riots of 1991, and *Twilight: Los Angeles* (Marc Levin, 2000), about the riots following the acquittal of the police officers involved in the beating of Rodney King in 1992. Her acting always maintains a clear distinction between the actor and the character, even though she reproduces verbatim the statements she collected in her interviews and maintains all of the interviewees' mannerisms.

This visual minimalism, whereby we are always and only looking at her, affords the possibility for the competing grievances she is voicing to be heard in their own terms. At first, the effect is visually challenging because, when looking at her, one has the uncanny impression of a body ventriloquized by an array of different voices. By maintaining this productive mimetic distance—by employing mimicry strategically— Deavere Smith is able to voice a multiplicity of grievances, many competing against one another. A particularly intense example from *Twilight: Los Angeles* is the moment when she reenacts one of the Simi Valley jury members' recalling, with tremendous grief, that the Ku Klux Klan invited him (or her, we don't know) into their fold after the verdict. As terrifying as this moment is, we can appreciate how Deavere Smith's technique resists the logic of passing as equation in favor of an effort to assure the equality of the positions she reproduces.

To be successful, her technique requires the suspension of identity politics. Hers are not impersonations—she does not appropriate someone else's grief—but citations. The effacement of her own identity can be seen as a strategy to *unfold identities in space* in order to mimic the possibility of multiple points of investment (rather than identification). At the same time, this effacement points to the refusal for racial grief to be located in any one specific place, person, or racial identity. Instead, she develops an ethical relationship toward her characters, given how precisely and respectfully she can voice their concerns, rage, or grievances, whether she agrees with them or not. In this process, Deavere Smith's blackness *passes* into something bigger than itself. It loses its particularity and becomes a more capacious signifier that is no longer tied to a specific identity, subject position, or social predicament.

Whiteness, as Robyn Wiegman has shown, is affected by the "paradox of particularity," that is, the fact that it passes as a universal category and commands the aesthetics and the form of universality only as a result of its ability to exclude— "for whites only."³ We can perform film analysis by looking for signs of the process whereby whiteness draws a line around itself and we can also think productively about whiteness as an orientation because the issue of a body in space is already implied in the way the cinema stages relationships between the human figure and her environment. Melodrama, in particular, is a genre that often highlights this relation.

The most influential exploration of how the melodramatic form has allowed American popular culture to process its own relationship to the "moral dilemma" of race relations is Linda Williams's *Playing the Race Card: Melodramas of Black and White from Uncle Tom to O.J. Simpson*. For Williams, melodrama characterizes the ability of popular cultural forms to elicit sympathy toward the suffering of certain characters as opposed to others, for example, the suffering white woman at the hands of a black man (Flora in *Birth of a Nation* or O. J. Simpson's wife) or the suffering black man at the hands of white villains (Uncle Tom). Melodrama offers a form for the articulation of injury through what is commonly described as "the race card."[4]

Alongside this reading, a critical race analysis might find useful tools in an understanding of melodrama as following the logic of commodity exchange to stage the incommensurability involved in any representation of equivalence. Melodrama relies on and enacts outrageous exchanges between things in order to point to the realm of the sacred, the individual, and anything that exists beyond, or that should be kept untouched by, economic exchange. For Agustin Zarzosa, melodrama showcases "the struggle between systems of exchange that compete to determine value."[5] This approach is clearest in his reading of Jane Campion's *The Piano* (1993), where two competing types of marriage (one understood as the exchange of women between men and the other as an exchange of vows between a man and a woman) institute two different logics, which are then negotiated throughout the film by means of a series of other exchanges involving piano keys, fingers, sexual favors, voice, muteness, and so on.

Todd Haynes's *[Safe]* (1995) suspends this logic of exchange and poses the problem for melodrama of the unaccountability of suffering, since the reasons for Carol White's illness are never explained. Carol is a white Southern California woman who develops some type of environmental allergy and leaves her husband and stepson to move to an enclosed desert community—the Wrenwood Center—away from environmental pollution where, however, her illness continues to progress. The film ends with Carol in her "safe" house, a sort of bare and fully enclosed igloo, trying to commit to self-love as key to her healing. She looks at herself in the mirror, which is instead the camera itself, and repeatedly says, "I love you."

The silence as to the real reasons behind Carol's illness allows the film to shed suspicion to the idea of injury itself, and it is through this move that the film acquires relevance as a formal critique of whiteness. As philosopher Charles Mills argues, the possibility of standing apart from the outside world, of even doubting its existence or the existence of other minds, is the prerogative of the Cartesian subject, which has to conceptualize itself as the very foundation of its own world. The Ellisonian subject (i.e., the subject represented by Ellison's invisible man) is, instead, in no position to "doubt the existence of the world and other people, especially that of [his] oppressors."[6] *[Safe]* encloses the character in an increasingly suffocating manner by building a narcissistic circularity on the idea that the only person who can make you sick is you. In this way, the film dramatizes the implosion of the Cartesian subject, which is invested in its own self-containment, and presents the melodramatic logic of exchange as a destructive exchange with oneself, whereby self-acceptance and self-sufficiency become yet another autoimmune reaction.

This conclusion underscores the partial efficacy of flipping the script—practicing the assertion, "Look, a white!" as philosopher George Yancy has done—which is a way to act as a mirror for whiteness and, therefore, to potentially show whiteness to itself.[7] Yet, this mirror function cannot help undoing the privileges of whiteness because whiteness, as Yancy also observes, is a way to deny the *actual* world and create an alternative world—a world where, for example, there is only one person and only one mirror, like in Carol's safe house. Thus, rather than looking for the source of Carol White's injury and indulging in what Zarzosa has described as the danger of the film, that is "the danger of becoming enamored with the suffering it purportedly battles," a critical race analysis might focus on how her orientation creates a white world within which she positions herself as injured and how this very injury can only result from the bankruptcy of the Cartesian self-sufficient subject.[8]

A focus on whiteness as orientation would produce a formal reading of the relationship between the human figure and her environment, and it would highlight how Carol's space has taken on the connotations of her own whiteness, including the fact that whiteness is what "lags behind" the body; whiteness is what "white bodies do not have to face."[9] Consistent with such a reading, the film opens with a traveling shot taken from a camera mounted on the front of the car in which Carol and her husband are traveling. The shot follows them as they cruise through an upper middle-class neighborhood in the San Fernando Valley toward the safety of their bourgeois home. In the next scene, she is having intercourse with her husband. The camera is high above the bed and shows, straight-on, only her condescending and resigned face. She accepts her husband's orgasm and pats him on the back. Her complacency with her gender role in the bourgeois family structure is visualized in the same way as the closing image of the film.

Carol doesn't work but defines herself as a "homemaker," which aptly, although unintentionally, describes the world-making capacity of her whiteness. She does not perform any tasks around the house, but, with the noise of a vacuum cleaner running in the background seemingly all the time, the film keeps the viewer aware of the labor required to maintain her sterile environment. Fulvia, her maid, gets called often, and for the most futile reasons, particularly because Carol does not know where anything is around her house. She can't find her phonebook, and, when she is told where it is, she hits her head on the side of a table while fetching it. We could interpret this as a sign of her incipient illness, or we can see it as a by-product of her orientation. From the exact location where she hit her head, Carol asks Fulvia for a glass of milk. She drinks it while sitting motionless at the vanishing point of her living room, in the very middle of the architectonic space and at the center of the film frame, while her "help" is busy laboring in the kitchen situated just behind her and to the side.

Lee Daniels's *The Butler* (2013), instead, puts "the help" at center stage and activates the melodramatic logic of exchange in favor of a different social critique that unfolds by experimenting with the possibilities and limitations of the cinematic imagination of social equality. Similarly to the way *Precious* (Lee Daniels, 2009) employs the main character's fantasy sequences to test its audience's assimilationist imagination, that is, its ability to accommodate that type of character and body within American visual culture, *The Butler* develops a visually glamorous family melodrama as an allegory of the nation's ability to fulfill its democratic promises.[10]

The film opens with its conclusion, as Cecil Gaines (Forest Whitaker) is sitting in a hallway at the White House waiting to be received by President Obama. He is shot from a high camera angle at a far distance. A cut to a medium shot shows him turning his head slowly to the left to look at a black guard standing beside him, and another slow tilt of the head in the opposite direction initiates a fade into the image of a double lynching unusually located in an urban setting. In this way, the White House's "help" is immediately framed within a narrative of racial progress. This framing can easily be construed as condescendingly liberal, but a critical race analysis might be able to identify edgier ways in which the film performs the social critique involved in adopting the epistemic advantage of the disenfranchised position while sharing the same visual lavishness normally reserved for upper middle-class whiteness, as in Douglas Sirk's melodramas.

The narrative begins on a cotton plantation in Georgia in 1926 with a scene that is narratively and visually equivalent to chattel slavery: the young "master" comes to the field to claim Cecil's mother (played by Mariah Carey), rapes her in a nearby shack, and, when Cecil's father reacts with a "Hey!" after prompting by his son, he is shot point-blank in front of Cecil's eyes. The sequence introduces the term "house nigger," which is used throughout the film as a chiasmus—a rhetorical or literary figure in which words, grammatical constructions, or concepts are repeated in reverse order—and therefore a productive site of exchange. Upon hearing the gun shot, the mistress of the house comes to the field and tells Cecil that, from now on, she will have him in the house and will train him to be a "house nigger," that is, train him to serve. The second time Cecil uses the term to reassure his prospective employer, a future mentor, that he is skilled at serving. The black man slaps him: "It's a white man's word, a word full with hate," he says, "Didn't your father teach you any better?"

When Cecil interviews with the White House *maître d'*, he puts into practice his mentor's suggestions to "look into their eyes. See what they want. See what it is they need," but also to "use those fancy words I taught you." After he does, the *maître d'*, satisfied, looks at him and exclaims, "Oh, yes, you'd make a perfect house nigger."

From this point onward, the film develops the tension between dignified manhood implied by Cecil's professional achievements and the militant manhood represented by his son Lewis's involvement in the Civil Rights movement and, later, the Black Panthers. At a purely formal level, this chiasmic structure sustains the film's dialog with the lavish aesthetics of melodramas of whiteness by making sure that the butler's house looks just as glamorous, commanding, and dignified as the White House. The film's glossy cinematography carries out the logic of melodramatic exchange *in favor* of a *visual equation* between the two dwellings as a prelude to a consideration of circumstances within which social *equality* between the first family and the first family's help can possibly be imagined and represented.

Consistent with previous projects, in *The Butler* Lee Daniels employs celebrity actors to play various US presidents and other roles in the film in order to keep the viewer aware of the film's deliberate artifice, along with the episodic and staged nature of the narrative. Almost without fail, every president (from Dwight Eisenhower to Ronald Reagan) shares both a moment of utter embarrassment and a moment of attempted equality with Cecil: each president gets "out of character" and seeks Cecil's insights into the ongoing civil rights struggle.

The comparative possibilities of parallel editing are similarly enlisted in the attempt to create a scenario of visual equality in the sequence that joins together the preparation for an official dinner at the White House, sit-ins at a segregated lunch counter in Nashville, and a training session for nonviolent tactics. The sequence has the same fast-paced, highly dramatic contrast as the famous baptism sequence in *The Godfather* (Francis Ford Coppola, 1972) but is here used to construct the idea of stillness as a civic virtue. The sequence follows a Student Nonviolent Coordinating Committee (SNCC) meeting at Fisk University, where civil rights activists are being trained in passive resistance modeled after Gandhi's techniques. The group's leader ushers in the sequence by explicitly announcing its cinematic nature—"It's show time," he says—and the sequence begins with a long shot of a dining room at the White House; just visible through the door frame in the back of the room are two pairs of white-gloved hands. The editing alternates between the activists entering a Woolworth's store and the butlers entering the dining room. The activists sit at the lunch counter, and a close-up of a plate being served to a white costumer is intercut with close-ups of gold-rimmed plates and golden silverware being laid out on the dining table at the White House. An off-screen voice says, "You know you can't sit here," over a panning shot onto the faces of the activists, as Cecil's son, Lewis, says, "We would like to be served, please"—a line used as a refrain for the rest of the sequence. Juxtaposed to a vertical shot of a perfectly arranged plate and silverware at the White House, the SNCC leader's voice-over asks, "Now, who wants to role-play?," again foregrounding the explicitly cinematic nature of the sequence. At the training session, one group of activists pushes and shoves another group that is practicing sitting still in their chairs without reacting to the abuse, while the leader continues, "Attack!" and demands the use of the word "nigger" as part of the training.

As violence escalates at the lunch counter, the sequence juxtaposes the stillness of the butlers standing in wait with extreme close-ups of tableware and the stillness the activists maintain while being abused. While an angry mob orders them to "get up," the film cuts to the White House dinner's guests standing up to acknowledge the entrance of the president. At the White House, the butlers help the guests take their seats while, at the lunch counter, activists are being pulled from their stools and kicked on the floor. A sound bridge of Lewis's cry of pain connects the image of hot coffee hitting his face with a slow zoom onto the stoic face of his father standing by, to the side of the dinner table, ready to serve.

The entire film is devoted to the narrative of progress that culminates with the Obama election, which Cecil Gaines is able to witness, while the butler's domestic situation is implicitly taking place against the backdrop of the first African American presidential family. In this case, the melodrama of black and white coincides with the coming of age of the nation and its fulfilment of the project of social equality envisioned during the Civil Rights movement. The point here is not to criticize the embellishment or glamorization of the Civil Rights struggle but rather to appreciate this formal and aesthetic exercise in *cinematic* equality.

Blackness made

It would be provocative, but possibly also accurate, to say that *Bamboozled* is the blackest film ever made. This is the case visually but is also revealed in the way the film showcases how blackness has been built throughout the history of US media; visual, material, and consumer culture; and the history of the senses. As Harry Elam writes, the "performance of niggerness" in the film signifies "a particularly American politics of belonging, a democratic appeal to a specifically racial, uniquely American denominator."[11] In turn, Stephen Best has shown how the stereotypicality of Harriet Beecher Stowe's characters in *Uncle Tom's Cabin*—their predictability, their commonsensicality—makes them unavailable to be secured as intellectual property. Instead, they are *Pro Bono Publico*, that is, they belong to the public and are for the public's free use.[12] Briefly put, *Bamboozled* shows how this *commonsensical* blackness builds a people, organizes their sensorium, produces images of common sense, and belongs to the public. Two implications deserve further attention. The first concerns the mobility that blackness acquires in the process of being commonly made; the second regards the repercussions this common "making" of blackness has on the question of representation. At the center is the relationship between the detachment of blackness from the body and the detachment of the body from representation.

In recent Critical Race Theory, blackness is increasingly discussed in relation to affect because affect offers a way to talk about this double mobility, that is, the fact that the growing representational mobility of blackness goes hand in hand with its detachment from the black body.[13] *Bamboozled* shows well how this detachability of blackness performs as a social lubricant and a glue that produces cohesiveness around itself. But, we might think of it also from the opposite point of view, as a possibility for the black body in the field of vision to be something other than just black. Simply put: does blackness ever leave the black body when it moves on its own? And more importantly, does its movement set the body free?

The conversation that has occurred around "postblack" art since the 2000s explores the possibility of unmooring both the black artist and the black body from the politics of representation. Postblackness puts pressure on the idea of a postracial society and describes, among other things, a refusal by contemporary artists to be bound by the limitations of identity politics and their critique of how the "blackness" of black art is deployed as its only principle of intelligibility. In reaction to the sociological imperatives of identity politics, postblack art champions opacity, ambiguity, illegibility, obliqueness, irony, and queerness in the effort to free artistic production from the same overdetermination to which the black body is subjected.[14] In other words, postblack art challenges the notion of a specific connection between one's identity and the content of one's art; it also unmoors "black" art from the obligations implied by the ideas of "speaking for" and representation as proxy. The cinematic image that is not subservient to the expectation of realism can attempt a similar unmooring.

The body unmoored?

Jim Jarmusch's *Ghost Dog: The Way of the Samurai* (1999) is a richly intertextual film that weaves together influences from eighteenth-century Japanese culture—in particular, the *Hagakure*, that is, the code of the samurai the main character lives by—Blaxploitation cinema, Kung Fu movies, the gangster film, and French film noir (through its reference to Jean-Pierre Melville's *Le Samurai* [1967]), among others. Structurally and aesthetically, the film is built on the formal traits of hip-hop music and culture and, in particular, its aesthetics of mixing, sampling, layering, looping, and over-dubbing.[15] RZA, a member of the Wu-Tang Clan, composed the film's soundtrack, and briefly appears in the film, which is full of other musical references. Ghost Dog, played by Forest Whitaker, lives by the code of the samurai and, because of this, has professed absolute fidelity to a low-level Italian wise guy. The man is part of an anachronistic and pathetic mafia family that meets in a Chinese restaurant (whose rent they cannot afford) and who are addicted to Golden Age cartoons.

The film adopts an overarching aesthetics of noncoincidence, whereby its protagonist offers an unlikely embodiment of all these various intertextual references, and triggers a series of formal displacements that coalesce around him. The latter occurs specifically as the protagonist's point of view and movements are unmoored from his body, and his body is unmoored from the image. From the beginning, Ghost Dog is associated with bird-like mobility. The film opens with a bird's-eye view over urban sprawl—quickly attributed to a flying pigeon that eventually lands on Ghost Dog's rooftop, where we find him reading from the *Code of the Samurai* and meditating on impending death (a meditation the *Code* says should be performed daily by imagining a variety of death scenarios). This list of death scenarios conjures up the image of a variously dismembered body and, thus, evokes a subject who is already a ghost and already corporeally beside himself.

Ghost Dog cannot go where the pigeon flies, yet the film pursues this evocative association through mobile shots clearly taken from his point of view but without anchoring them to the image of his moving body. The dramatic crisis of the film, which turns the Italian family against him, occurs when Ghost Dog is contracted to kill Handsome Frank while his mistress is unexpectedly present as well. In disdain, she throws the book of *Rashomon* on the floor, and, when Ghost Dog arrives and shoots Handsome Frank, he notices the mistress and the book and stops in his tracks. She tells him that it is a good book and that he can have it, since she is done reading it. Ghost Dog takes it. The camera is on her and then cuts to a tracking shot to the left that leads outside the room from the point of view of Ghost Dog; however, this is not followed by any shots anchoring the camera movement to his body.

Ghost Dog is associated with mobile points of view—long car rides, long tracking shots—but also with the untethered mobility of sound. He often initiates diegetic music by playing his boom box or CDs in the cars that he effortlessly steals and then drives with white gloves. Moving invisibly through the urban space, people around Ghost Dog seldom acknowledge his presence; in a few instances, people who happen across his path move around him so closely as to almost brush up against him, yet they do not seem to notice his presence. There are some notable exceptions, including his best friend, an ice-cream vendor from Haiti. He speaks only French, and, even though Ghost Dog speaks only English, they communicate perfectly with one another. Another exception is Perline, a little girl who strikes up a conversation with Ghost Dog under the pretext that he talks to no one and has no friends. Finally, a dog twice sits still in front of him and stares. Only RZA stops in his tracks to greet him.

Ghost Dog's movements are only partially captured by the film image and, therefore, always virtually mobile beyond what we can actually see; when he moves through space (for example, from the background to the foreground of the frame) his body disappears and reappears through brief dissolves. Yet, his movements still maintain an integral quality, even when they appear and disappear within the frame. When he practices martial arts on his rooftop, his body fades in and out of the image through a combination of slow motion and dissolves. Still, as much as the body is literally untethered from the image, the effect of the body's movements and the trajectories of its gestures still linger within the image.

This fact sets him dramatically apart from the Italians, who are instead characterized by a mummy-like fixity, awkwardness, and lack of dexterity, or animated movements similar to the cartoons they watch obsessively. Sonny, who can be regarded as Ghost Dog's *doppelgänger*, becomes particularly animated at every mention of hip-hop culture such as rapper's names and, especially, their music (Sonny's favorite, he says, is Flavor Flav, and he immediately erupts into a rap, to the consternation of Mr. Vargo, the mafia family's head). Although he limps, Sonny does not refrain from dancing and singing along to his favorite Flavor Flav song, "Cold Lampin' with Flavor," just before Ghost Dog flawlessly kills him.

So, if the Italians stand on the side of animation—an animation that is partly fueled by blackness—Ghost Dog clearly stands on the side of the cinematic: the moving image lets his body, as well as his "ghost," float untethered to spatial and temporal constraints. In this sense, the film fully embraces the possibilities of hip-hop aesthetics, with hip-hop as the "first culture that has broken loose of rootedness and that can exist, intact, while mobilizing blackness independent of black corporeality."[16] The insistence on deploying signifiers that don't seem to land on their expected references ultimately creates a textual field where Ghost Dog can move freely and choose his own course of action.

One of the achievements of *Ghost Dog* is to embrace the mobility of blackness, not in the direction of appropriation or impersonation, but for the purpose of organizing itself around an untethered black body. It encourages film analysis to seek the body that organizes the textual system—Carol's in *[Safe]*, Delacroix's in *Bamboozled*, for example—and to be keenly aware that invocations of the human sensorium in film theory, no matter the framework, are not race-neutral. In this sense, a critical race analysis offers ways to *flesh out* cinematic bodies beyond the accounts provided by phenomenological approaches, body genres, or theories of cinematic excess. Critical Race Theory can offer some insights into alternative ways to think about the "body politic" of the cinema—that is, to think about blackness as that which fills the space in between people, bodies, and things in a way that is ethically binding.

Ultimately, however, the detachment of blackness from the body and of the body from representation still constitute unequal scenes of exchange, and Critical Race Theory pushes film and visual culture studies to investigate these imbalances. As Harry Elam argues, contemporary culture has demonstrated the capacity for blackness to detach from the body and circulate on its own apart from black people; indeed, this is so prevalent that it is increasingly "easy to love black cool and not love black people."[17] This double movement, therefore, poses a pressing ethical question about the possibility of loving black people alongside "loving" blackness. It does so in part because neither of these two movements is real: Ghost Dog's mobility does not exist in the real world. In public spaces, presence, real movement, and even the perception of movement are still dangerous, still constructed as a threat that can be eliminated with deadly force. This is the question that Critical Race Theory ultimately poses for film studies, that is, the question of the relationship between the fungibility of blackness and the political ontology of the Black as a human subject and a citizen—a relationship that unfolds in the cinema through the visual fact of blackness.

Notes

1 Michael Gillespie, "Smiling Faces: Chameleon Street, Racial Passing/Performativity, and Film Blackness," *Passing Interest: Racial Passing in US Novels, Memories, Television and Film, 1990–2010* (New York: SUNY University Press, 2014), 257.

2 Due in part to this deliberate instability, *Chameleon Street* had difficulty finding distribution and received a lukewarm, when not indifferent, critical reception. As a "black film"—"black" because of the identity of its writer, director, and star actor—it was unlike any other film made within the 'hood genre that began in earnest in 1991. Thus, *Chameleon Street* was met "with the consistent refusal to rethink the idea of black film." Yet this is one of the film's greatest achievements, that is, the fact that the instability and mobility of blackness pursued by the character precisely matches the instability of the label of "black" film. Gillespie, "Smiling Faces," 272.

3 Robyn Wiegman, "'My Name Is Forrest, Forrest Gump': Whiteness Studies and the Paradox of Particularity," in *Multiculturalism, Postcoloniality, and Transnational Media*, ed. Robert Stam and Ella Shohat (Brunswick, NJ: Rutgers University Press, 2003).

4 Linda Williams, *Playing the Race Card: Melodramas of Black and White from Uncle Tom to O.J. Simpson* (Princeton: Princeton University Press, 2001).

5 Agustin Zarzosa, *Refiguring Melodrama in Film and Television: Captive Affects, Elastic Sufferings, Vicarious Objects* (Lanham: Lexington Books, 2012), 71.

6 Charles Mills, "Non-Cartesian *Sums*: Philosophy and the African-American Experience," *Blackness Visible: Essays on Philosophy and Race* (Ithaca: Cornell University Press, 1998), 8.

7 George Yancy, *Look, a White!: Philosophical Essays on Whiteness* (Philadelphia: Temple University Press, 2012).

8 Zarzosa, *Refiguring Melodrama*, 64.

9 Sarah Ahmed, "The Phenomenology of Whiteness," *Feminist Theory* 8, no. 2 (2007): 156.

10 Alessandra Raengo, "Shadowboxing: Lee Daniels's Non-Representational Cinema," in *Contemporary Black American Cinema: Race, Gender, and Sexuality at the Movies*, ed. Mia Mask (New York: Routledge, 2012), 200–16.

11 Harry Elam, "Spike Lee's *Bamboozled*," in *Black Cultural Traffic: Crossroads in Global Performance and Popular Culture*, ed. Harry J. Elam, Jr. and Kennell Jackson (Ann Arbor: University of Michigan Press, 2005), 355.

12 Stephen Best, *The Fugitive's Properties: Law and the Poetics of Possession* (Chicago: University of Chicago Press), Ch. 2.

13 Tavia Nyong'o, "Unburdening Representation," *The Black Scholar* 44 (2014): 70–80; Derek Conrad Murray, *Queering Post-Black Art: Artists Transforming African-American Identity after Civil Rights* (London and New York: IB Taurus, 2015).

14 Darby English, *How to See a Work of Art in Total Darkness* (Boston: MIT Press, 2007); Derek Conrad Murray, *Queering Postblackness* (London and New York: I. B. Taurus, 2015).

15 Eric Gonzalez, "Jim Jarmusch's Aesthetics of Sampling in *Ghost Dog: The Way of the Samurai*," *Volume! La revue des musiques populaires* 3, no. 2 (2004): 109–21.

16 Derek Conrad Murray, "Hip-Hop vs. High Art: Notes on Race as Spectacle," *Art Journal* 63, no. 2 (2004): 18.

17 Harry J. Elam, Jr., "Change Clothes and Go: A Postscript to Postblackness," in *Black Cultural Traffic*, 386.

FURTHER READING

On Critical Race Theory:

Frantz Fanon, *Black Skin, White Masks*, trans. Richard Philcox (New York: Grove Press, 2008). This is the foundational text for understanding the visual "fact of blackness." It has also grounded a theory of film spectatorship and thus it is the necessary starting point for considerations of race in the cinema.

Ian Baucom, *Specters of the Atlantic: Finance Capital, Slavery, and the Philosophy of History* (Durham, NC, and London: Duke University Press, 2005). This book makes one of the strongest cases for the imbrication of race and capital while exploring the implications it has for our concept of time, history, and the way the afterlife of slavery still haunts our present.

Richard Delgado and Jean Stefancic, *Critical Race Theory: An Introduction* (New York: NYU Press, 2012). This is written specifically for a general audience and it outlines CRT tenets very clearly. It includes helpful pedagogical exercises.

On the making of race:

Anne Anlin Cheng, *The Melancholy of Race: Psychoanalysis, Assimilation, and Hidden Grief* (Oxford and New York: Oxford University Press, 2000). Racial melancholia offers an indispensable tool to think about entanglements of fear, desire, disgust, attraction, intimacy, and oppression in everyday interactions. It also offers an important key to understand the obstacles and challenges to the effective completion of the assimilationist project championed by the Civil Rights movement.

Mark Smith, *How Race Is Made: Slavery, Segregation, and the Senses* (Chapel Hill: University of North Carolina Press, 2006). This is the first book to undertake a sensorial history of race.

Very clearly written, the book is indispensable to begin to think about race as a form of articulation of the human sensorium.

Toni Morrison, *Playing in the Dark: Whiteness and the Literary Imagination* (New York: Vintage Books, 1992). This is one of the most influential sustained critiques of the purported racelessness of the American literary canon, which maintains its "whiteness" because it "chokes" the presence of its racial others. Morrison's close readings of canonical literary texts offer effective and accessible models of critical race analysis.

W. J. T. Mitchell, *Seeing through Race* (Cambridge, MA: Harvard University Press, 2012). Mitchell is one of the most prominent visual culture scholars, and in this book he leverages the visual conceit underlying both the idea of double-consciousness and the "fact of blackness" to propose that race should be understood as a medium.

Critical Race Theory in film studies:

Alice Maurice, *The Cinema and Its Shadow: Race and Technology in Early Cinema* (Minneapolis and London: University of Minnesota Press, 2013). This book offers a successful example of Critical Race Theory as film studies. It identifies the central role of race in the development of the film medium, especially as it concerns the translation of the performing body into the performing image. It shows how, from the beginning of the cinematic apparatus, the "shadow" of race was understood as a problem of form.

Ella Shohat and Robert Stam, *Unthinking Eurocentrism: Multiculturalism and the Media* (London and New York: Routledge, 2014, 2nd edition). This a pivotal book to think through the question of representation. The book offers a plethora of flexible tools for "multicultural" analyses of the way racial and power relations are encoded in media texts as well as analytical strategies to make sure that submerged minority voices can be successfully heard. Equally importantly, it showcases, in an accessible manner, a very large body of non-Eurocentric critical theory.

Kara Keeling, *The Witch's Flight: The Cinematic, the Black Femme, and the Image of Common Sense* (Durham, NC: Duke University Press, 2007). Building on Gilles Deleuze's notion of the *cinematic* to underline how cinematic perception extends beyond moving image media and involves the construction of social reality, Keeling investigates how "blackness" constitutes an image of "common sense." The goal of the book is to challenge commonsense images to configure alternative ways of imagining social relations.

INDEX